COACHING
FOOTBALL
SUCCESSFULLY

Bob Reade
Augustana College, Rock Island, Illinois

Human Kinetics Publishers

Library of Congress Cataloging-in-Publication Data

Reade, Bob, 1932-
    Coaching football successfully / Bob Reade.
      p.   cm.
    Includes index.
    ISBN 0-87322-518-X
    1. Football--Coaching. I. Title.
  GV956.6.R43 1994   93-1272
  796.332'07'7--dc20   CIP

ISBN: 0-87322-518-X

Acquisitions Editor and Developmental Editor: Ted Miller
Managing Editor: Jan Seeley
Assistant Editors: Moyra Knight, Dawn Roselund, and Lisa Sotirelis
Copyeditor: Merv Hendricks
Proofreader: Karin Leszczynski
Indexer: Barbara E. Cohen
Production Director: Ernie Noa
Typesetter: Julie Overholt
Text Design: Keith Blomberg
Text Layout: Tara Welsch and Denise Lowry
Cover Photo: Fred Marzolph
Interior Art: Tom Janowski and Tim Offenstein
Interior Photos: Fred Marzolph, Dennis Collins Photo, and Greg Boll/*Quad-City Times*
Printer: Versa Press

On the Cover: Augustana College All-American tailback Brad Price breaks a tackle en route to a touchdown in a 1986 NCAA Division III national championship semifinal game. Augustana Coach Bob Reade (in photo at right) and his team went on to win their fourth consecutive national title that year.

Human Kinetics books are available at special discounts for bulk purchase. Special editions or book excerpts can also be created to specification. For details, contact the Special Sales Manager at Human Kinetics.

Printed in the United States of America

10 9 8 7 6 5 4 3 2

Human Kinetics Publishers
P.O. Box 5076, Champaign, IL 61825-5076
1-800-747-4457

Canada: Human Kinetics Publishers, Box 24040, Windsor, ON N8Y 4Y9
1-800-465-7301 (in Canada only)

Europe: Human Kinetics Publishers (Europe) Ltd., P.O. Box IW14, Leeds LS16 6TR, England
0532-781708

Australia: Human Kinetics Publishers, P.O. Box 80, Kingswood 5062, South Australia
618-374-0433

New Zealand: Human Kinetics Publishers, P.O. Box 105-231, Auckland 1
(09) 309-2259

Dedication

This book is dedicated to the girl I married 32 years ago, Mary Jo, and to our eleven children—Kelly, Robin, Tracy, Kristin, Barry, Mark, Erin, Whitney, Ryan, Molly, and Kyle, the "Home Team."

Contents

Foreword

What great timing! Just when colleges and high schools are considering cutting back on and even eliminating football programs, *Coaching Football Successfully* provides a strong case for our sport. And no one can make a more convincing argument than Bob Reade, whose high school and college programs have been the epitome of academic and athletic excellence for more than 30 years.

Many of you know about Bob's incredible winning percentage, 60-game win string, and four national championships. But what's more important is that Bob has accomplished these achievements through proper values, discipline, and humility. That's why Augustana is the furthest thing from a "football factory," and yet its win-loss record is the envy of every school that has tried to build one.

Coaching Football Successfully is must reading for all coaches at all levels. Players and their parents should also read it, not just to learn more about the game, but to reconsider football's role in their lives.

The beauty of Bob's book, like his teams' performances, is in its impeccable organization, apparent simplicity, and flawless execution. Its major strength, however, is not its looks but its substance. Bob addresses every coaching principle, from planning through evaluating.

If you're looking for Xs and Os, you're in for a treat. In addition to presenting a variety of formations, plays, skills, and drills, Bob takes you through the thinking process of developing an offensive attack and a defensive scheme. Moreover, he explains the process of teaching players the techniques and tactics they must execute in game situations.

Coaches like Bob Reade are the backbone of our profession and our sport. Read *Coaching Football Successfully* and refer back to it often. Better yet, read it often and challenge yourself to coach by its standards.

Joe Paterno
Penn State University

Acknowledgments

No one person can accomplish success alone, and any measure of success you may attain cannot really be enjoyed unless you can share it with those around you.

To acknowledge all the people who have helped me over the years to reach any level of success would take at least a separate chapter, but I do want to recognize and to thank a special few.

First and foremost, I want to thank all the fine young men—and the parents of these young men—that I have had the pleasure to teach and coach. I feel that as a coach I have been blessed with the greatest of all talents, and without these players' efforts there would have been no teams.

To the coaches who have assisted me both in high school and in college, especially Tom Schmulbach, now assistant head coach and offensive coordinator at Augustana, and Larry Johnsen, defensive coordinator. The three of us have worked together for 20 years both in high school and in college coaching.

Thanks to them and to all the other coaches who unselfishly gave their time and effort to help build and maintain our fine football program.

To Merle Harris, the finest high school coach I ever met, who gave me my first responsibility as his assistant coach in Maquoketa, Iowa.

To the great men who also happen to be great football coaches throughout the country who opened their minds and their playbooks to help me learn the game of football.

To Ted Miller of Human Kinetics for all his encouragement and his expertise in preparing this book for publication.

To my parents, to Mary Jo's parents, Joe and Mary Manning, and to all of our children for their love and support through the good times and the bad.

And to Leo Cabalka, a high school coach who took special interest in me and guided me into the coaching profession.

Introduction

Six years ago my daughter Robin gave me Harold Kushner's *When All You've Ever Wanted Isn't Enough*. This may be the finest book I have ever read. Kushner says that in a life there are three things a man should do: Have a child, plant a tree, and write a book. So *Coaching Football Successfully* completes the trinity.

Before Ted Miller of Human Kinetics approached me about writing this book, becoming an author was far down my list of priorities. And when I learned how long the book was supposed to be, I had even less interest in writing it. Family, coaching, and teaching already filled up my days. How would I ever have time to put a book together? It seemed impossible, but here it is!

This is not a typical football coaches' book—it's not strictly biographical or simply Xs and Os. Instead, it's a combination of the two, a wedding of principles about life to an approach for coaching football. To my way of thinking, even the winningest coach is successful only if his program reflects proper values and operates within the rules.

I believe very strongly in what the first four chapters of this book stand for. If you read nothing else, read Part I. You might not agree with everything that's said about coaching philosophy, communication, motivation, and building a football program, but at least you'll be thinking about these topics—the foundation for any long-term success in our great sport.

The next section, on planning, describes how to plan for the season and for practices. We all have different ways of planning, but there are some basic guidelines to follow, and the most basic is that every coach must plan.

In Part III you'll find football techniques, tactics, and drills for coaching offense, defense, and special teams. Several types of formations and strategies are presented, but our Augustana Wing-T offense and 5-2 Rover defense are highlighted. Here I do more than just show the diagrams. I also explain when a particular skill or strategy might be applied and how to teach it.

Everything that goes into preparing for and coaching games is discussed in Part IV. Here I stress that games are really decided during Tuesday through Thursday practices. I also emphasize the importance of players' focusing on and enjoying each game.

The last section is on evaluating players, teams, and your total program. It involves more than just looking at statistics and wins versus losses. Evaluation is the key to improving the attitude and performance of your players and coaching staff.

As I finish this introduction, I'd like to clarify one thing. The use of the word "I" is never very comfortable for me. But through the editor's insistence, this singular pronoun was used instead of "we" in various instances throughout the book. I'm embarrassed that in some cases I may come across like a know-it-all. Please believe me when I say that I am neither a know-it-all or a do-it-all. Coaching football, like playing the game, is a *team* endeavor.

I have been fortunate to have great assistants and great players in our programs. And as a result we have enjoyed great success at the high school and college levels. Yet we don't pretend to have all the answers. So what you'll find as you read *Coaching Football Successfully* is simply what has worked best for us. I hope you find something in the book that will work for you too.

Part I

Coaching
Foundation

Chapter 1

Developing a Football Coaching Philosophy

When I first entered coaching, the things that concerned me most were how much talent I had on the team, what kind of size and quickness we'd have, whether my strategies would work, and what kind of opponents we'd face. I soon learned that those things are secondary when it comes to being a successful football coach.

First, you must have a base—a philosophy or foundation to which you can refer to make decisions. So before I cover the Xs and Os in this book, I am going to share with you some ideas regarding a coaching philosophy for football.

I believe that football is a team game to which Christian principles apply: You work together, play hard, obey the rules, and treat everybody as your equal. When faced with tough coaching decisions, make sure to base your choices on those important principles. It is because I believe such values can and should be advanced through sport that I continue to coach.

Two Keys to a Successful Coaching Philosophy

All successful football coaches have a solid foundation to guide them. Here are three prerequisites for building that base:

• *Know yourself.* Are you essentially a close-to-the-vest type of guy, or are you a gambler by nature? Perhaps you fall somewhere between the two. If you don't know where you stand, reflect on the five most important decisions you've made in the past 2 weeks. What were they? How did you feel after making them? By answering such questions you'll better understand what makes you tick.

• *Be yourself.* Everyone has heroes. But too often coaches attempt to copy a "big-time" coach's style or use a winning coach's "new" strategy. I don't recommend either approach *unless* the style or strategy is consistent with the way you already approach your work and your life.

• *Be honest with yourself and others.* Coaches who think they can fool others, and particularly their players, aren't very successful and don't hang around long. Shoot straight—the least you'll have is your integrity, and probably a long career as a coach as well.

Know What You Want to Teach

Before anything else, you must know who you are and what you want to do. As for myself, I've always loved games. Football is a game, and I love it. So coaching lets me stay close to something very dear to me.

Some coaches, unfortunately, have taken the "game" away and made football a business. At whatever level I have coached, I have kept it a game.

Probably the most important thing about my own personality that has led to any success I've had as a football coach is summed up by that old saying: It doesn't really matter who gets the credit, just so the job gets done. I've always emphasized that team concept.

In football, more than any other sport, you need the person next to you and he needs you. A head coach needs his assistants; a quarterback needs his offensive line. Whereas a Michael Jordan can dominate a basketball contest, it takes a combined offensive and defensive *team* effort to dominate a football game.

So think first in terms of the team, and encourage all of your coaches and players to do the same. That is the driving force behind a successful football program.

Examine Your Philosophy

My start in coaching was a typical one. I was fortunate to begin work as an assistant to Merle Harris, the finest high school coach I've ever known. But like many of you assistants who are reading this book, I wanted to climb the ladder.

So I hurried to get ahead in the coaching ranks. After being head coach at a small school for a few years, I moved to a larger school. I then realized the importance of having a sound philosophy and began to appreciate coaching for itself rather than always searching for a better position. About the same time, I realized that the joy of helping each year's team accomplish its goals, not the size of the school, is the real thrill of coaching.

 A SPECIAL MOMENT

One of the happiest times I've had as a coach, and the most joyful I've ever seen a team, was not after a state or national championship, but rather in my first year as a head coach when my team won its first game after two winless seasons. The players on the team never dreamed of winning a game. We had only 16 players on the team, even including freshmen and sophomores as part of the varsity. But let me tell you, there wasn't a dry eye on the bus after we won that game. To see players who acted like whipped dogs in our first practice—never really believing they could succeed—be so excited and joyful over what they had accomplished together was, and always will be, very special.

Such experiences helped shape my philosophy just as they shape yours. Because of these experiences, for the the last 30 years and for the remainder of my coaching career, my primary coaching objective is this: *to help bring a group of young men together each season so that they play as well as they can as a unit and have respect for each other.* It sounds simple, but I find it the most challenging and rewarding part of coaching.

It has become more apparent to me over the years that the relationship between cohesiveness and respect among players is vital to success. A strong team consists of players who feel responsible for each other's success; they simply won't let each other fail. If you create such an awareness and teach your players to perform well together, you will fulfill what I believe is a football coach's most important job.

Maintain Your Perspective

I urge you to keep football a game. But remember that this game can offer valuable learning experiences to those who play it and coach it.

If you treat players like machines who are only as valuable as the number of wins they produce, you'll deny them the enjoyment of the game that they deserve.

Too many coaches have it backward, thinking that winning is necessary to build a team spirit or cohesiveness. I've never worried too much about the winning and losing; the record takes care of itself if you attend to team building first.

The Three Fs

To keep football in perspective, I tell my players to prioritize their responsibilities, using the three Fs:

1. Faith
2. Family
3. Football

The Fellowship of Christian Athletes is important to me because it keeps these three Fs in perspective. It's not easy to keep them in order, so when you are consumed with football problems, step back and try to remember that the sport is third on your list.

Faith. You can't preach or push your beliefs on others. But as I've coached I have found that successful living is based on a strong faith—faith in God, faith in the player next to you.

Good teams always have that faith. Each player believes the guys lined up next to him will do their jobs and not let the others down. That's the faith I'm talking about: Every player does his very best.

Family. Football should never come before family. Because I believe Sunday is a family day, I never ask my team or coaches to meet on Sunday. Coaches, players, and players' parents should have one day free to do anything they want. Sundays and holidays are precious times to be spent with loved ones.

Football. Football is third among the three Fs, but if you are a member of a football staff or team, it has to be important to you. You must be ready to pay the price for it.

When we hit the practice field, I want players to know we mean business. We are going to work you, teach you, praise you, scold you, and run you. We want your best effort. Give it your all, and then when you leave you are back to your other pursuits, to your life beyond football.

Only a few of the players we coach are going to make their livings as athletes. We sometimes forget that. If you take every day of a kid's life for 4 years, you've deprived him of many life opportunities and freedoms. You're saying you know better than he does what he should do during off-season. Over a 4-year period, by calling all the shots for him, you can significantly delay his maturation. Think about it. Remember, he's going to be a person and perhaps a parent a lot longer than he's going to be an athlete.

As a coach, it's your responsibility to guide your players and to try to make being on the team the greatest experience of their lives. If they choose to go on to another level of football, that's fine, but it's important for them to have a full high school experience. You can see to it that their football-playing days are good ones.

Be Yourself

I always tell students in my psychology of coaching class that they can't try to be somebody else. You can't be Don James or Don Shula; you've got to be you.

Still, we are an outgrowth of everybody we have met and admired. So learn from the John Woodens and Vince Lombardis, just

as you learned from your parents and others you respect. But don't kid yourself into believing that just because something worked for Joe Paterno it will work for you.

 BO DID IT HIS WAY

Bo Schembechler was a controversial football coach at the University of Michigan, sometimes losing his cool on the sidelines and at postgame press conferences. He'd throw his headphones, berate officials, criticize the media, and point his finger at athletic programs he believed were cheating. Whether he was right or wrong, that was Bo. He was honest in his approach to the game. He was honest with the fans and the media. And, most importantly, he was honest with his players. That's why they respected him so much and played so well for him. They knew he was being totally up-front with them and that they all would be treated fairly.

It's funny but true that the ideas that you or I pick up from other coaches are ideas consistent with our own. When a speaker says things you agree with, you're likely to think it was a great speech. Conversely, if you disagree with the speaker, then you're likely to think it was a terrible speech. We tend to be attracted by—and to more readily understand—things that are consistent with our philosophy. If you are conservative by nature, you'll be more likely to incorporate something from another conservative. We can change ourselves only so much. Then

we have to make the best of who we are, and understand that others won't always agree with what we say and do.

 THE PLAYER BECOMES COACH

I was never a great player, but I was a thinking player who knew his responsibilities and tried to execute them as well as possible. I always believed my mental concentration and preparation for the game were important to my performance, and I still think so as a coach. As a player, I never cared for or engaged in "hot-dog" behavior. In some ways, I coach like I played. I discourage players from showing off, because such actions bring attention to the individual, not the team. I'm glad to see some rules being changed to penalize such behaviors. The spotlight should be on the team as a group, especially in football.

Make Your Philosophy Work

Anybody who says your team's win-loss record isn't important hasn't coached or played football. So I won't even waste time talking about the significance of winning. But coaches, players, and parents who have winning as their *only* objective are misguided and far too narrow in their focus.

When you prioritize winning, fun, and development, the key thing to understand—and make sure that players and their parents understand—is that if your athletes play as a team and enjoy what they are doing, they will win. So, everyone associated with the program should focus on the prerequisites to winning, *team play* and *effort*, instead of the outcomes of games. Teamwork and effort come when a coach effectively teaches skills and strategies to players and when players build their desire to play the game. Success in football depends on many people coordinating their roles, each doing the right thing, together.

Developing Players

I believe in starting with basics. Teach players fundamental individual techniques and team concepts, and winning will take care of itself. Also emphasize values that are the backbone of any program that experiences long-term success.

Practices can't always be fun. Practices are hard work. You have to emphasize that the real fun comes on Friday night or Saturday. In other words, fun comes at kickoff.

In preparing for a game, my emphasis is on teaching—helping players learn—for coaching is teaching. Teach in a way that lets players understand and makes them believe. Also be consistent in your teaching.

Making It Fun

When the season is over, you should see some development in your players' physical, mental, and social skills. You should also see that they have had an enjoyable time, because they've spent too much time with you to dislike what they're doing.

If football is a game to you and your players, and if you allow them to play it as a game and not label it a life-or-death activity, then it should be fun. And without question the most fun comes when a team has spent itself with effort and has been successful in the game.

Notice that I said "been successful" and not "won." The two often occur simultaneously, but success always can be within your control and your players'; winning depends, in part, on the opposing team's performance.

Practices, although involving a lot of work, also can be fun. I like to inject humor and variety into workouts when I think it is appropriate. Keeping players upbeat and interested helps them learn much better and encourages them to give greater effort during workouts.

Certainly, the number of games you win will influence how much the players enjoyed the season. But after the season's over, they'll most miss the rewarding experiences they had pursuing those victories.

Winning Perspective

I put little emphasis on victories because they are a *result*, not a *goal* in itself. And winning in part depends on the performance of opponents. Players already hear enough about victories or losses from parents, classmates, and fans. So direct their attention to developing their football skills, their enthusiasm for playing the game, and their effort. Instead of merely looking at the win-loss record, have them ask two questions:

- *Did I play as well as I can?*

- *Did we as a team play as well as we could?*

The outcome of a game is secondary to individual performance, teamwork, and effort. In fact, I've probably scolded teams more after wins than after losses. That's because we have won some games on superior ability even though we played poorly. It's important that the team realize after such a game that it regressed by playing poorly, regardless of the score.

Share Your Philosophy

So the question is, "Do you base your season on a 9-0 record or on playing as well as you can?" If you base it on the win-loss record, the odds are stacked against you: Few programs go undefeated for even one season. But if your team plays as well as it can and loses to a better team, you can still feel successful.

The real value of a good win-loss record is that it helps sell everyone on your philosophy. If you are fortunate enough to win in your first year or two, people in and around the program will get excited and will generate a positive momentum going in the direction you want. Lacking that momentum, they may be less willing to accept what you have to say.

Share Your Philosophy With Players

We tell our players before the season that we may lose, but not the same way twice. Meaning: Learn from your losses and mistakes. That's one of life's lessons players can take from football. I'm not saying you have to lose to learn that lesson, but you need to make players aware of errors that they might not correct themselves.

That's why we scold some teams after a victory: We don't want to lose a game later because we developed bad habits while playing sloppily but still winning.

Share Your Philosophy With Assistants

You must be confident your staff agrees with your approach because you can't have two philosophies. If you do, you'll have disharmony among the coaches. Players must know that the assistants are working for the head coach and that chain of command must remain intact.

A staff that cooperates and believes in your philosophy helps matters function smoothly. I've been fortunate to have a great coaching staff—all good coaches and good friends—that works together and has genuine interest in the players.

Share Your Philosophy With Parents

As a coach, I feel a responsibility to the players' parents too. While coaching in high school I realized that I was spending more time with many of my players than were their parents. So I saw an important responsibility to pass on my positive values and to strengthen their commitments to school and to the team.

    ABOUT COMMITMENT

A parent once asked me after the season: "How do I get my boy to be as good a boy after the season as he was during the season?" I told him that his boy was committed to football and to the rest of the team, he wasn't committed to me. I believe that a big part of coaching is to emphasize dedication, sacrifice, and positive attitude. When you do, it's amazing how much some players will develop as people.

Some coaches hold preseason meetings with players' parents to explain their coaching philosophies. I've always believed my actions and the players' actions were effective enough means through which I could communicate my philosophy. Although it's more difficult to "walk the walk" than to "talk the talk," it strikes me as far more effective.

Teach Life Values

I have great respect for the title "Coach." Being a head coach or an assistant coach and bearing the responsibility for the players' well-being is an awesome job. But it's also a great opportunity. For you, as a coach, can help teach your young people the disciplines of life.

John Wooden is the greatest coach who ever lived. The values he passed along to his players were grass-roots, life-long principles. Sometimes, though, his players were reluctant to accept what Coach Wooden was preaching.

 A LESSON FROM THE WIZARD

The great Bill Walton had long, shaggy hair before his senior season started. Someone asked Wooden about the free-spirited center, and how he was going to discipline him. Wooden is to have said, "That's OK if Bill wants his hair long, he just won't play basketball for UCLA with it like that." He didn't get on a high horse and threaten Walton, he just stood by his principles and said if the best player in college basketball chooses to abide by the team's rules, fine. And, if not? We'll never know. Bill Walton got his hair cut to specifications. And today he would tell you that he benefited from that simple lesson on teamwork—one of many Wooden taught his players.

I was a high school football coach, teacher, and dean of boys (aka chief hind-end kicker) during the '60s when discipline went out of style. My approach was to be absolutely *fair* no matter which kid got in trouble. Repeat offenders tested my fairness, but it's interesting to note that as those people—regular visitors to my dean's office—matured as adults, they became some of the most gracious people I know.

They realized that I tried never to give them any more or less than was coming to them. I guess they must laugh about how they used to write my name on the wall and call me names that aren't fit to print. But, apparently, with that laughter comes a deep respect for being treated fairly.

 MORE THAN A HAIRCUT

Team unity rules can teach valuable lessons. One player of mine in particular resisted the rule we had in the late '60s about hair length. Today he is a successful lawyer in Illinois. But, while interviewing for a law firm intern position, he was told that to get and keep the job he would have to wear a suit and tie every day and keep his hair short. His parents told me, "You know, it's kind of neat he'd heard that before and realized that conformity is sometimes necessary."

Threat to Values

The professionalism of sports and the emphasis on the entertainment dollar in sports have crept all the way down to the high school level. As a result, in too many cases, the only thing that is acceptable to the school administration and fans is winning.

That focus on winning means lots of people are willing to sacrifice values for it. Pro teams will draft someone in the first round even though he's a convicted felon. Colleges will recruit "blue chippers" who have no business in an academic environment—just to keep the TV and alumni money rolling in. And now you see it in high schools that offer enticements to junior high talents.

Conference championships now are almost meaningless and state championships have lost some of their allure. Now it's the *national* title that everyone wants. Even in Little League, the World Series title is the rock candy mountain.

That's all destroying a value. And we are getting used to the corruption. People barely flinch now when an NCAA champion is found to have sidestepped the rules on the way to its title. What we've said is "It's OK to cheat and win" or, the inaccurate and cynical outlook, "Well, everyone else is cheating, so why shouldn't I?" A coach who adopts either perspective is not teaching or upholding important values.

Coaching and Cheating

The paradox, as I've noted, is that if you don't win, few will believe in the things you do to help your players develop and have fun. Therefore, you won't get much support from parents, community, or school. Nobody will say to your players, "Hey, you're really doing well." And kids want and need that kind of reinforcement.

You can teach all the great fundamentals, but if you don't win, you'll hear from everybody who thinks they know more about the game than you do. Eventually, if you lose too often, you'll be asked to resign.

So do you cheat to get better players or bend the rules? Absolutely not. If you have to cheat to keep a job, step back and think whether the job is worth it to drop your standards that low. Is it worth it to show your players that kind of example? And if you get caught, is it worth it to always carry the cheater's label?

If you're at a school where the win-at-all-cost philosophy thrives, ask yourself if you have helped promote it. Do you cut corners, bend rules, hold secret, out-of-season practices? If so, you deserve what you get when the program crumbles on top of you.

The absence of values in sport is why the dynasty program is so rare. The UCLA and Green Bay dynasties had values throughout them that were extensions of their coaches. They are proof that a sound foundation is important. Anybody can put a bunch of outlaws together that are so good nobody can beat them one year. But if a team doesn't have a solid base—a shared philosophy among the coaching staff and the players—then it will soon have problems with discipline and it will erode from within.

Win on More Than the Scoreboard

It's really a tragedy that everything—at least the judgments of most fans and the media—is based on the score. Years ago, as a speaker at a Fellowship of Christian Athletes Weekend of Champions in Fort Dodge, Iowa, I said that the biggest fault of high school sports is the scoreboard because the scoreboard immediately tells everybody who won or who lost, but it says nothing about team or individual performances. The "losing" team may have played its best game or a player may have performed way above his ability, but still the side with fewer points on the scoreboard is labeled a loser. Yet the other team, the "winners," may have played below its ability and given half the effort. So you tell me who *really* wins, the team or player who gave an all-time best effort and "lost" or the team or player who went half-speed and "won"?

The winning-is-the-only-thing phrase isn't true. What's most important is going into a contest and giving maximum effort. You are in a position to teach your players this basic principle and many other values related to teamwork such as dedication, sacrifice, and discipline.

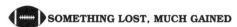 **SOMETHING LOST, MUCH GAINED**

Sometimes it's not easy to stand by your convictions. For example, in 1982, the year we finished

second in Division III, we suspended 4 of our top 48 players before going to the semifinal game in the playoffs. It was a hard decision because it meant we'd be without a leading rusher and some key defensive players. And it may have cost us that national championship. But I'm convinced that my sticking to the philosophy in making that harsh decision had much to do with our winning the next four national championships.

Football is supposed to be a game, involving fair and honest competition. And as a coach it is your job to see that you and your team take that approach. Sure, we go at each other as hard as we can. But after the game, we accept the result and get ready to do better the next game. We feel good about competing because we're playing on a level field. But if you play outside the rules, then I can't accept it.

Be a Model of Your Philosophy

Players need good models of character. Unfortunately, there seem to be fewer athletic heroes that young people can model.

We expect our players to be good role models, to give kids who look up to them good examples to follow. A more selfish reason is that my sons have all been ballboys since they were old enough to hold a football; I want them to have good role models. Therefore, our players *and* coaches, including me, must lead by our actions.

It's just vital for a coach to set a proper example. Your personal and professional demeanor will have a big impact on your team's discipline. You are a professional. You can't "talk" one game and "walk" another.

Two Points of Emphasis

If I had to narrow to two points what to look for from players, they would be effort and teamwork. The teams that play hard and play as a team will never disappoint you. As we explain to our team, it comes down to understanding the difference between *should* and *could*. Every team wins all it *should* win, but not necessarily all that it *could*.

Summary

1. I firmly believe that a coach's philosophy and teaching ability will be more important than which formation his teams line up in before the snap.
2. I urge you to think through your philosophy and to include in it the teaching of sound values.
3. It has been my experience that these teachings are the most rewarding and lasting part of our teams' success.

Chapter 2

Communicating Your Approach

As educators and coaches, we can teach *and* learn only if we are effective communicators. Successful coaches both send and receive information clearly and efficiently. Coaches must interact effectively with

- players,
- assistant coaches,
- game officials,
- fellow coaches,
- players' parents, and
- media.

I hope this chapter will help you get along with these and others you deal with. We are all different; what works best for me may not for you. And yet the most important principle of communication—treating others with respect as you speak, listen, and observe—applies universally.

Successful coaches are leaders, and they know how to effectively communicate their leadership. Furthermore, they know how to promote leadership qualities in their players.

Communicating *With* Players

I've always preferred the term talking "with" rather than talking "to" players. The former term reflects a give-and-take; the latter suggests a monologue.

Players will teach you things, if you watch and listen to them. Because we as coaches communicate so many things with our players, some intentional and some not, and under so many circumstances, I'll focus on three important types of interactions:

- *Personal*: concern and respect
- *Philosophical*: character and model behavior
- *Professional*: practice and game

Communicate Concern

When talking with players during the off-season, it is important to show individual concern. Ask them about their family, their schoolwork, and their general well-being, not just about their last workout. It's necessary to communicate to players that they are important to you not just as football players but as people.

Communicate Respect

The player is the most important person in the program. He must be treated with respect and dignity by every coach. You may scold him from time to time, but don't belittle him, insult him personally, or embarrass him. Think of each football player as special, whether he's an All-American or a first-year player just hanging on. Each player has sacrificed to be on the team, and each has attributes that make him special.

You can't treat the star player as more special than you treat the least-talented player on the roster. It's naive to think players don't know their pecking order; that fifth-string player knows he's fifth string. But you have to communicate to all players that they are important to you and to the team.

Communicate Your Philosophy

In chapter 1, I emphasized the importance of establishing a philosophy. The key to putting that philosophy into action is communicating it effectively and consistently to players. Always emphasize that football is a game, not life and death. But add a reminder that players must practice and play all-out.

  THE ONLY WAY

One year we had a letter winner, a starter, coming back who had worked in the weight room all winter and spring. Then, in the fall during two-a-day practices he didn't really work. It was apparent that he was waiting for the season to start playing. He would just go through the motions. I talked with him and said, "You're not working; what's the matter?" He replied, "I'll be there, coach, I'll be there." I told him to look at how the other players were working and advancing.

When it came time to pick our traveling squad, I just couldn't put the young man on the bus. He hadn't earned it. And yet I knew that he could play better than the guy who was playing.

He ended up quitting. I didn't want him to quit because he could contribute, but to give in to him would be unfair to the others.

There's no doubt we could have won that day's game. But we wouldn't have won the national championship, as we did, if I had endorsed that player's indifferent attitude.

You have to stay aware of players' efforts. But you should always encourage players to monitor themselves, asking these two basic questions:

- *How well did I play?*
- *Am I playing as well as I can?*

Obviously, players will have bad days, but what you need to watch is when a player has frequent "off" days.

We try not to play people on the basis of their potential, but rather on what they have done. So our starting lineup is not determined by a size chart or a speed chart, but rather by good performance and good effort. That instills in the entire team—from top to bottom—the attitude that to play they must work and improve.

Communicate Character

Character is taught by example. You are asking for honesty from each player. You are asking him to get in at night on time, to be at practice on time. You are asking for straight answers from him. If you teach him that cheating is OK on the field, how long will it be before he starts cheating off the field too? By teaching illegal acts you destroy a fundamental value, one that is hard to get back once it's lost.

Some coaches tell their players, "This is the way to hold and not get caught. I know it's illegal but this is the way we are going to block it." After saying something like that, does the coach have any right to expect honesty from those boys?

Today's young people learn soon enough that "getting by with things" is OK. You should want more than that for and from your players. You want them to be the best they can be.

 WOODY MEMORIAL

It's unfortunate that one of the greatest coaches of all time is remembered by so many fans as the coach who threw a punch at a Clemson player out of frustration. Certainly that act was inexcusable, but Woody Hayes, the late Ohio State University Coach, deserves better because he was a far better person than what the public ever knew.

Woody's former players have been unanimous in their praise. That's because Woody never publicly singled out anyone for criticism. For instance, he took the heat from the media for kicking a star player off the team, rather than explain that the kid showed up drunk at an awards banquet. Woody just said the player had broken a rule, never taking the player's dignity away and maintaining his loyalty to the boy. The player came back the following year, worked harder than ever, and became an All-American. Woody gave him that second chance.

Character and discipline must be taught. We are born without either. We believe we can discipline ourselves, but that's not true. As a coach, you need to give players patterns of life and disciplines that will help them until they're ready to accept more of life's responsibilities.

Foul Language

Many football coaches, players, and fans use profanity. I don't like it, but I also recognize that there are two different types of profanity.

Vulgar profanity includes the word "you" and is directed at another person. The other type of profanity is used almost like slang during an outburst, and isn't intended to hurt anyone.

Neither form of foul language is right, but to me there is a great difference between the two. And I've always thought that distinction was important, because one expression is intended to harm another person, and the other is slang caused by frustration.

Communicate as a Model

I've always believed in the phrase "More things are caught than taught." If I want discipline and I don't want foul language or poor behavior, then I have to set the standard. I can't ask players to be neat and well-mannered and not provide a good example. What I expect of them, they can expect of me in return. I make that clear from day one.

You have to live it. That doesn't mean we have to be saints, or that we should expect our players to be perfect. But we have to be willing to subtly correct actions that would have a negative effect on the team.

Communicate About Education

The focus of a football program must be education. In my opinion, the college presidents, through the NCAA, are trying to put "college" back into "college athletics."

Propositions 48 and 42 were designed to send a message down through the colleges to high schools and to junior high schools: "Son, you've got a full college scholarship, but only if you can get into college by earning a high enough grade point on core courses and a certain score on the college entrance examination." So instead of spending 30 hours out on the field practicing football, the boy spends 15 hours there and 15 hours studying. He can have both his athletics and his academics. This straight talk also helps him realize that we are interested in his life, not just his football.

The emphasis on academics must come from the top of the pyramid: the coach. Work with young men to help them understand their schoolwork is important, preceding even football in importance. Everyone will soon get the message that academics are emphasized in your program.

Let them know the responsibility is theirs. That is a good learning experience for young people. They need to know there will be no rule bending. Those who change grades or give athletes breaks send a poor message.

Communicate During Practice

I'm not a big lecture coach. The only thing I'd lecture on is mental attitude. In other words, I talk with players about concentrating—what they need to think about, what keys to watch for—to see that they are focused on their responsibilities.

We do most of our teaching on the field. We prefer to walk players through the chalk talk. I'd rather show them and have them run through the offensive or defensive tactics. We have few all-lecture classroom practices.

I don't believe a player can learn a skill by reading or by listening to a lecture. You can read Jack Nicklaus' golf book over and over, but you won't develop the perfect swing unless you practice it.

I'm a practice coach, and I prefer to have a team of practice players. Coaching strategy communicated at the proper time can win games only if the adjustments have been practiced correctly and repeatedly.

Communicate Football Techniques and Tactics

Communication involved in teaching a skill involves three steps. You first explain to the player how to do it, then show him how to do it, and then walk him through it. Then you start it over again, explaining, demonstrating, and guiding him through the technique.

 BACK TO THE BASICS

Folklore has it that after a rare loss by his Green Bay Packers, Vince Lombardi was particularly upset with his team's many fumbles. So Lombardi demonstrated—to one of the all-time great pro teams—the most basic fundamental: holding a football. Here is one of the most respected professional coaches in football teaching an experienced pro running back how to hold the ball when running with it, just as a Pop Warner league coach might show a 10-year-old beginner. One of the Packers' team clowns, watching the coach proceed with this instruction, sarcastically said, "Slow down, you're going too fast for me."

If players seem to make the same errors, maybe you failed to communicate effectively the skill or strategy. Go back to the basics and walk your player through the skill again. And don't think that players understand something just because they nod their heads when you explain and demonstrate it.

Communicate Positively After Errors

A word that I emphasize, especially in practice, is "but," as in, "That's a great effort, *but* here's the correct way . . ." You reinforce the good things and scold the things you'd rather not see. The key is to have a positive component to the message.

If all you do is yell when a player makes an error, he may not even realize what he did wrong. But you'll definitely hurt his pride. So use "but" when correcting errors, especially with players just learning the skills of the game.

Consider trying nonverbal communications with players. Gestures—a smile, a wink, a shake of the head—can express more than words. Facial expressions often are the best way to communicate privately—just you and the athlete know. That way you aren't embarrassing the player in front of 1,000 or 5,000 people.

Communicate During Games

A key to coaching well is communicating effectively during games. You must have a system simple enough to allow for quick adjustments you need to make. Halftime is too late to make adjustments. So during practices, make sure players understand important options that vary from your base offense and defense to handle special situations. And find simple ways to communicate those changes during the excitement of games.

Communicate at Appropriate Levels

Obviously, you cannot deal in the same way with players who are at different stages of development. A coach must communicate at his players' level.

You must realize each group's skill level and, maybe even more important, determine why the players are out for the team in the first place. A junior high boy is not participating for the same reasons as a high school player. A high school player probably is playing for different reasons than a college player.

Potential Obstacles to Communicating With Players

- Coaches who are indifferent about the value of communicating. They do not make an effort to communicate with their players.
- Coaches who force athletes to communicate in a prescribed style, thinking their players are a reflection of them.
- Coaches who are so concerned with impressing players with their knowledge of the game that they don't talk *with* them.
- Coaches who are poor teachers. They can't teach exactly what they want and neglect proper instructional steps.

Communicate With Staff Members

I do let my staff coach. It's vital to give an assistant coach the freedom and authority to make decisions. Not only will this make him work harder, but he'll also get more respect from the players he works with because they'll see he has responsibility. If he's not a good coach, not coaching the way you would like, or doing something inconsistent with your beliefs, it's in your team's and his best interest to let him go.

 ASSISTANT COACHING DAYS

I remember my first day as an assistant coach for Merle Harris. Boy, was I excited. I was the line coach, and he was the backs and the head coach. So my expectations weren't too high in terms of responsibilities. As the team concluded calisthenics, Merle talked to the players for 10 minutes, then said, "Line, go down there with Coach Reade, and backs, come up here with me." Now, to my surprise, I'm all of a sudden solely in charge of the 30 line candidates who were jogging down the field with me. I'm their coach. My first day ever on the field as a coach and I was given full responsibility for half the team.

The nice thing about that was from that day I knew I had a period during each practice that I was line coach and during that period of time I was the *head coach* to those players. Thereafter, from the time I left practice I would begin getting ready for what I'd teach the next day.

I had to prepare. The head coach would assign the time to me and tell me certain areas to work on, but then turn it over to me. I liked that tremendously, and I spent as much time away from the practice field preparing as I would if I were head coach for my segment of time.

Assistants should not be clones of the head coach, but I want assistants who have similar philosophies. That's important when it comes to communication. If assistants contradict the head coach's philosophy, who will the players believe?

That doesn't mean they need to agree on every part of the game. For example, my defensive line coach may have an aggressive approach to the game. My offensive coordinator may be more analytical and calm in demeanor. Assistants may differ in personality, but it is important that they share a concern and respect for all players and promote your philosophy day in and day out.

Just as you should not put down a player in front of others, you should never put down an assistant coach for making a mistake. A former principal taught me never to say anything demeaning to a staff member because that staff member would lose some of the players' respect.

Later, tell the assistant you would have handled the situation differently. Any good staff member would agree to that and work with the head coach.

Communicate With Game Officials

I believe all officials are basically honest. They make mistakes, but so do coaches. The big difference is that when they make mistakes, coaches rarely hesitate to complain.

In all the years I've coached, I've not gone onto the field more than a dozen times to chastise an official. When I have, it was for an obvious error in applying the rules that I felt could hurt the team.

The key to confronting an official is to have your say and then forget it. Don't let your emotion distract your coaching the rest of the game. Too many coaches complain at the end of the game about bad calls in the first quarter that they believe cost them the game. But if your focus was on the first quarter, how could you coach the team the last three quarters? You have only 48 or 60 minutes to succeed, so if you lose focus on the game, you lose time you should have used to help the team.

Another negative outgrowth is that when you start yelling, it's hard to keep the players from doing the same. When they start griping, they won't be concentrating on the game.

 CHANGING THE RULES

Geneseo High School still has records for penalties in the state playoffs, even though when I was coach there we weren't violating any rule as it was written. We used a hand signal to send our wingback in motion. In the playoffs one official started calling illegal motion on us on virtually every play, even though it was legal. I even had a letter from the head of the state high school association saying it was legal!

Later the state made it illegal to send a man in motion with hand signals from the quarterback. I'm very proud we executed well enough to make the state change the rules to stop us. We called it the "Geneseo Rule."

If you see something in a film of your opponent that you believe is illegal—holding or crackback blocks, for example—I think it's your responsibility to your players to talk to the officials about it before the game.

The reason we have football rules is to protect the players and keep the game fair. So, if you see something being done by the other team that violates a rule, it's your responsibility to let the officials know about it for safety purposes.

Before a game, officials will seek you out. They'll ask if you've got any special plays or have seen something on the other team that they should be alerted to. It's your duty to inform them fully.

Communicate With Other Coaches

I have great respect for the many great friends I have made among football coaches across the country. I really look forward to the American Football Coaches Association (AFCA) convention every year.

I think we have good communication within the coaching community. Joining the AFCA is a great thing for high school and college coaches. All the football coaches at the annual conference are willing to share information. If you sit in on a program where a coach talks about something you'd like to incorporate, he'll probably take time to answer your questions.

 STUDY TIME

When I was in graduate school at the University of Iowa I would constantly ask Iowa coaches if I could watch film. I was such a pest that they gave me a key to the film room. I didn't want to bother them, but I wanted to learn and watch. Watching the films—many of them several times—was really a great value to me.

I learned from those films, even though the style the team played was far different from the one I adopted. That's a lesson for younger coaches: Learn every system you can, because even though you might not use it, you'll likely face an opponent who uses it.

It used to bother me when college assistant coaches, who coached only one position, would come to the high school to recruit but couldn't answer questions about any other phase of the game. I think such specialist coaches are making a professional mistake not knowing other areas of the game, especially if they want to be head coaches.

That's the advantage a high school head coach has over other coaches: He has to know about all the positions on offense, defense, and special teams. It really gives you a broader picture of the game. So I am critical of the mental preparation of many young coaches who don't look beyond the defensive backs or receivers, for example. They lose sight of the fact that the performance of all 11, not just 4 or 5, players on the field is crucial to the team's success.

Communicate With Parents

My advice on communicating with parents is to make sure you first communicate well with the player. He's the key. If he's satisfied (he's not always going to be happy) that he's getting a fair shake, then he is going to take home a positive attitude.

Make sure the player knows he has been given an even shot. But, no matter how fair you try to be, some will always judge your actions as unfair. That is a very difficult thing, but you have to know yourself—your motives—and be certain that you don't play a young man because he's white or another because he's black; you don't play a young man because he's 6-4; and you don't play a young man because his name is Jones or Smith.

If players trust you and believe in your integrity, they will be your best ambassadors with parents. That comes from being consistent. You can't talk one game and "walk" a different game. Remember, you're teaching values along with football.

You are in the public eye and you have responsibilities to your community, school,

players' parents, and the players themselves. So you cannot just do as you please. You are going to have to exercise self-discipline—the same self-discipline you are asking of your players.

Although I said the player should be your first concern, don't get the impression that communication with players' parents is unimportant. If you are doing your job, you will be communicating with parents all the time. If you are true to your philosophy, you and the parents will share the same concern—the boy.

When parents come to you with a problem, be as honest as you can. Tell them what you are trying to do, and that your actions were not meant to hurt their boy. Demonstrate that you have their boy's best interests in mind. In turn, they should have faith that you will treat their son fairly and appropriately.

Suspending a player is a drastic measure. Sometimes, because the boy knows he did something wrong, he'll go home and say he quit rather than that he was suspended. I don't think it is my responsibility to call Dad or Mom with a different story. But if Mom and Dad want to talk to me, I feel comfortable telling them the truth and my reasons for making the decision.

 THIRD TIME'S A CHARM

Sometimes coaches—myself included—get little prejudices. I had a kid who came out as a sophomore and quit. He then came out as a junior and chucked it after 2 weeks. Finally, he showed up as a senior, and I said to myself, "A lot of good that's gonna do. What does he want to come out for?" You see, I was already mad at him for quitting twice.

So when he came for his equipment about a month before practice, he said, "I'll have to tell you, coach, I'm going to miss the first couple of two-a-days because my dad and I are going fishing." I thought, "My gosh, what is he coming out for anyway? It will last only about a week." But I said, "Fine, you have family responsibilities."

After the fishing trip, he showed up for practice. We were still having two-a-day practices, and one particularly hot day (probably 100 degrees) he played defense against our first-string offense. Well, during this scrimmage he just kicked the devil out of us. He did everything. We couldn't make a yard. And all the time I'm thinking that I didn't want the kid to make it.

In fact, I would have done anything to get rid of that kid because I was fed up with his past actions.

After practice, I saw this boy sitting on the cement wall near the entrance to the high school, soaked with sweat. After his performance, I had to say, no matter how much it hurt, "Hey, you had a good day." He looked up and said, "You know, I'm out here for one reason this year; my dad made me, but it's kind of fun." He ended up being an all-conference defensive player.

After you are a parent, you understand better that parents come from an entirely different perspective than do coaches. First, parents want their son to get the best of everything, and that can cloud their thinking. Second, parents see every move that boy makes in a game. You're watching the whole team, and until you see film you don't scrutinize each individual. Just as it's hard to see the faults in your own family and friends, it is hard for parents to see some of the faults in their own sons.

Coaching Your Son

I'll never forget the first day of practice with one of my sons on the team. It was kind of cute. He came up to me and wanted to say something while I was talking to somebody else. To get my attention he said, "Dad? Coach? Dad?" He didn't know what to call me!

Coaching your own son can be hard on you. But if you are sure you are playing him because he is the best player on the team at that position, then you should have no doubts. Somebody will always criticize you, and they are welcome to do that. But if the coaching staff and other players on the team are with you, then those detractors should be no problem.

It's also hard on a coach's son because someone will say he played because you are his dad. This is especially true when he is in close competition with another player for a position. I was fortunate in coaching my son, Barry, because he had perhaps the most objective skill in football—kicking. But he also played quarterback, which is a subjective skill position to judge and a position of high visibility.

It's important that your boy work hard and earn his peers' respect. He can never try to take advantage of his relationship with you. Some things you must keep as a parent-son relationship; others should be kept within the coach-player relationship. On the field at practices and games, interact just as if he were not flesh and blood.

A coach-son situation is also hard on the wife and mother. Imagine sitting in the stands while some guy next to you criticizes both your boy *and* you! The coach's wife hears all the bad things about her child and her husband. And the coach's other children also hear their father called a lot of names. I think fans forget sometimes that a coach's family can suffer from comments directed toward the coach.

 MORE THAN A FAMILY MATTER

My wife really kidded me after one game. We were ahead 40-0 when an opposing lineman jumped offside by a mile and blocked our extra-point kick. The officials called no penalty, which was terrible because he was so far over the line of scrimmage. Worse, he catapulted over another player, which also is illegal.

I was upset that an official was allowing the player to break two rules and call nothing. So I complained to him and he said, "What are you on me for, Bob? That isn't going to hurt your team. You've got it won."

I told him, "I know it doesn't make any difference in this game, but down the road that could cost us a national championship because someone like you doesn't enforce the rules."

When I got in the van to ride home with my wife, she turned and said, "Sure, your own son gets a kick blocked and you're out there arguing. Anybody else, you wouldn't be out there." She had to tease me right away because I must have looked just like an upset Little League father trying to justify his son getting a kick blocked.

Parent Meetings

I never held preseason parent orientation meetings. They are very popular now, and I see nothing wrong with them. If you coach in a metropolitan or suburban school, where you may not have frequent contact with parents, it may be a good idea.

A lot of good things can come from such meetings. Parents can meet you and hear your plans for working with their boys. Be yourself because you don't want them to get the wrong impression or expect you to do something you cannot fulfill.

Communicating With the Media

Publicity, when kept a positive influence, and not disruptive, can be good for your school. I can tell you that being the focus of attention has a positive effect on the school. During one football season—when things were going well—we had few discipline problems. The whole school rallied around the program. Even though they may not be athletes, students like to read positive statements about their school.

 CLAIM TO FAME

I grew up in a little town in northeast Iowa where folks bragged that they had the world's largest feather duster factory. As a kid I thought that was a pretty neat thing—to be the biggest in the world. Actually, the building was only about the size of a large house and since feather dusters have become a tool of the past, the building has been torn down. But I sure felt like it was important to be in a town that could make such a claim. The value of positive publicity, regardless of its origin, is something that everyone can feel good about.

Make sure that you present your program and school in the best possible light to the media. And, associated with that, be frank

and honest with every reporter you encounter.

Media Misdeeds

What disturbs me is when the media step out of bounds to sell papers or attract viewers. Perhaps the worst example of this was the overexposure given to former University of Oklahoma player Brian Bosworth at the 1987 Orange Bowl after he had been suspended for steroid use. All the media did was publicize something that was wrong. You don't win or lose a game with the guys who don't play. You win or lose with the guys who are playing.

The sports media also, at times, try to get into a coach's head. They insert their own answers to their questions. That isn't fair to the coach or the program.

 GETTING THE STORY RIGHT

I remember an article done years ago on our program in Geneseo. The focus of the story was the youth football program we had developed and its impact on the community and our varsity team. The story quoted me as saying, "Without the Little League program, our guys wouldn't even know how to put on their pants."

I would never say that. The writer had shot down my assistant coaches. I had a great freshman coach, sophomore coach, and JV coach, and he shot them down by saying they don't know enough to teach players how to get in their uniforms.

I apologized to each one of my assistant coaches. They knew that I would never say what was attributed to me, so that part of it was no problem. But what can you do to set things straight with all the other people who read the article?

Preseason Comments to the Media

Preseason forecasts are so hypothetical. All coaches have to say they are good or going to be good. That's the great thing about coaching—either your program is "there" or it is on the verge of getting there.

Preseason polls are guesses at best, based on schedules, returning players, and tradition.

You want football in the newspapers for the benefit of your sport. So you don't want to neglect the media, and I'll even admit to being disappointed when they haven't written about us.

To get media attention, some coaches will rate their current team in comparison to past teams. I never liked that.

One coach, when asked what his greatest team was, replied, "I haven't had it yet." I liked that because it didn't slight anyone who had played for him and put something up there for future teams to shoot for. I never thought you could compare teams; they play different schedules and have different players. So it's not fair to compare teams, and it's not fair to compare individuals.

 ANSWERING A DUMB QUESTION

When I started at Augustana, I didn't know how we would do because I hadn't seen the team play, and I didn't know the opponents' strengths and weaknesses. I had seen only about eight Division III games in my life! How would I know whether we could win? But sure enough, at the press conference announcing my hiring, a reporter asked, "How long do you feel it will take you to get the Augustana program going like you had the Geneseo program going?"

Well, to me that was a stupid question. I said, "I don't know if we ever will as far as winning is concerned. But I can tell you when the Augustana program will be as good as the Geneseo program: when everybody in the Augustana community likes our football program, respects our athletes for the type of people they are, and wants to come to see them play." That had nothing to do with winning or losing, but that was the only way I could honestly answer the question.

So, if someone at the preseason press conference asks how your team is going to do this year, give an honest answer based on your experience with the program and the opposition. Don't use the media to play up or put down your team.

Pregame Comments to the Media

The press always asks, "What's the team's attitude?" before an especially big game. I just say, "We are looking forward to it. We will be ready to play." That's the way I always feel. I can't wait to get started. Big games add even more excitement.

I don't make pregame predictions because I never feel going into a game that we are going to lose. Yet I always feel there is a way that we *can* lose. I always respect every opponent, but I've always had the confidence that if our team plays to its potential, it will win.

You may have read quotes before national championship games where I said, "We'll be okay if we play as well as we can play." I'm not being evasive. That is really my honest answer. Playing as well as you can defines winning.

Postgame Comments to the Media

I like a 10-minute cooling-off period after games, especially after a tense playoff game or a tough loss. It's a time when you should be with the team to celebrate or counsel.

With the media after a great win, you point out the things the team did well. If you didn't play well and won, be honest in your assessment. The players will read it and then hear it again on Monday.

Football is a team game, so focus your comments on the team. If somebody has a great game and did something individually that was critical to the outcome of the game, say so, but exercise caution to keep it in the team perspective.

One of the worst things you can do is to set one player apart from the team. So never say something like, "If the rest of the team had played as well as Jeff did, we would have been OK." That isolates Jeff from the rest of the players.

When Speaking to the Media

⊘ Don't put down another team or player,

⊘ Don't bad-mouth your own players, and

⊘ Don't discuss players' personal problems.

Also, avoid pointing out that the offense or defense played better. That creates two teams. When I came to Augustana, we had two teams. I kept hearing that the defense was OK but that the offense wasn't good. At the first staff meeting I said, "Let me tell you one thing right now: We don't have two teams here. We don't have an offense and defense even though we're two-platoon. We are in this thing together." The success of one depends on the success of the other.

Communicate Leadership

One of the most intangible and yet important things a coach must communicate to players is his ability to lead. I believe leadership must be in a pyramid arrangement, with the head coach at the top. The staff and the squad must realize that's how things are organized. You cannot assume they know it; you have to make it clear from the first time you meet with them. The worst things happen when the head coach does not back up his position of authority with effective leadership.

That doesn't mean it's all one way, from the coach down to his assistants and then to the players. I encourage input from my staff *and* players. Several times players have suggested ideas better than mine. I am always willing to listen to assistants' and players' recommendations, but they must have a good explanation of why their approach is better than the one we were going to use.

I always look to develop assistants' and players' feel for the game. Because of their positions, quarterbacks and defensive backs often see action on the field in ways that give them great ideas of strategies that might work.

Although this cooperative approach involves give-and-take, it must have a streak of authority behind it. Players must know that you are receptive to their ideas. If you stay open to their input and don't deal with them heavy-handedly, both you and they will benefit.

Leadership Styles

The authoritative style is abused too often and becomes a regimenting rather than a disciplining approach. If you are strictly a regimented team and don't have a cooperative approach, then frustration sets in when things fail. They say you know only the robotic approach. The cooperative approach

is much better because the player has the freedom to adjust a little bit on his own and not be so regimented that he thinks there is absolutely only *one* thing he can do. A cooperative style loosens the reins and gives players flexibility and options to do the job.

If you look at great programs—the Lombardi program and the UCLA basketball program—they are obviously led by good people. They had a central figure who everyone knew was in charge, and everything would revolve around him. That's important. Because the game moves so quickly, everyone must agree who's in charge so adjustments can be made in time.

Player Leadership

Player leadership on and off the field is vital. The style of leadership may vary, but it should always have cooperative and authoritative components. It should be cooperative to the point that input is welcomed, but authoritative enough that when the time comes, everyone jumps to the leader's command. Players can't question it. If a play is called, everyone must respond.

 TOO MANY CHIEFS

The thing is, on this team, there are so many smart kids. They all know the automatic system as well as the quarterback knows it. In fact, in one of our national championship games, our guard and tackle kept telling our quarterback he ought to check off on a certain play. This upset the quarterback, so he called timeout and came to the sideline and explained what the linemen said. After that series of downs, I got the offense together and said, "Just listen to him," as I pointed to the quarterback. "When the quarterback calls the play, just do it. He's the leader."

Some leaders are born, others are made. Some people have a natural ability to lead because they are gifted players and are ready to make the play. God gave them the talent. They are leaders by abilities. Other players lead by intelligence. They know the game, they study the game, and they think quicker in the game because they work harder than others.

The best leaders are leaders on and off the field. Good leadership takes place in the classroom, the locker room, and on the practice field.

On-the-Field Leadership

Leaders push others to greater heights. They give their greatest effort and encourage teammates during practice, after practice, and throughout the game. Leaders must be able to do what they are telling their fellow teammates to do. Leaders don't just talk, they provide examples for others to follow.

When you have good leaders, it helps you as a coach. It's hard for a coach to assume the leadership role in every area because he is usually too critical about little things. Then, when big things come up, the bark has no bite.

The quarterback is often looked to for leadership because he calls the plays in the huddle, checks off, and is in a position to see everything. So sometimes leadership comes, by default, with a position.

Off-the-Field Leadership

In some ways it is more vital that your players exhibit good leadership off the field than on the field. You only see the players on the field maybe 3 hours a day. If a player doesn't have any commitment to you and to the values that you put in football, there is no way in 3 hours you can teach enough to counteract what he picks up in those other 21 hours.

Summary

1. You can't fake communication.
2. You must be a people person. Some of the things I've mentioned here will help, but even more importantly, you need a genuine interest in others. From that point you can develop the communication skills to do the job.

Chapter 3

Motivating Players

I am often asked, "How do you get your players to play so hard all the time?" And that's something I have never been able to answer in a conversation or at a coaching clinic. But here's my chance: an entire chapter about motivating players! It's the key to success.

If everyone knew how to motivate players to their optimal levels at all times, physical talent and Xs and Os would determine a coach's success. We'd all be equal. But because motivation is such an elusive aspect of coaching, it is the ability to motivate players that distinguishes successful coaches from less successful ones.

The Basics of Motivation

As coaches, we think that high school football players should be self-motivated. That type of motivation comes from a player's inner drive. It's the kind of motivation every coach looks for but the kind only a few players have. Therefore, football coaches like you and me are always looking for ways to increase players' desire to play and contribute to our teams.

My motivational approach isn't derived from complex psychological theory or the latest pop psychology. I am too practical and too old for such approaches.

Instead, my beliefs about motivation come from what I *know* works and what doesn't work. Foremost among those beliefs: *You can't make a player do anything, you can only make him want to do it.* So that's what we try to do, that's our goal. And to accomplish that goal, I think a coach needs to do three things.

1. *Get your priorities in order and convey them consistently.* Your ability to motivate is

25

very much dependent on your philosophy (chapter 1) and how you communicate it to others (chapter 2). A sure way to spur motivation is to let athletes see that their well-being is always a primary concern. Conversely, a win-at-all-cost approach dictated to players through one-sided monologues will do little to motivate them.

2. *Show interest in every player and let each know that you are trying to help him improve.* It may sound simple, but players need to believe that *your* coaching motives are also in their best interests. Your efforts to improve their physical, social, psychological, and emotional skills will elicit greater effort from your players.

3. *Learn the general principles of motivation.* In this chapter, I will explain what I think are basic ways to motivate players. In summary:

- Be positive.
- Set goals.
- Be consistent.
- Provide discipline.
- Set an example.
- Avoid complacency.
- Punish rarely.
- Give players a say.

Be Positive

The best rule in working with players is to emphasize encouragement over discouragement, especially when you are building a program (chapter 4). You've got to be positive to get your players thinking positively. To succeed, they need to believe in themselves, and that's easier if they know you believe in them.

Avoid basing your reinforcement of players on the team's win-loss record. There's no problem praising players when their performance and record are good. And it's really fun to coach when everyone pats you on the back. But when things aren't going well, and the win-loss record reflects it, your encouragement of the players may decrease, and it may be harder to be positive. Players hear only about their mistakes, and so their motivation is either down or based on fear—neither of which are positive.

So, instead of outcome, praise and reward players depending on how they answer the question, "Have I done my best?" I reflect on this myself as I walk off the practice and playing field. And I expect each of my players to do the same. You shouldn't wait to answer until you see the film. You and your players should be able to answer that question before you reach the locker room. If you have done everything possible, you can hold your head up.

Players need to know that sometimes their best won't be good enough for the scoreboard. But they also should learn to take pride in their effort, independent of the score. And that pride will motivate them for a lifetime.

Set Goals

Great effort is helpful only if it is purposeful. Using goals gives players something to aim for—stepping stones to reach major objectives. After all, "No goals set, nothing really achieved."

Some coaches set goals because they sound good and make them look prepared. But worthwhile goals are easy to set, hard to meet. Be prudent in setting goals, and then be committed to reaching them. If you find they are unattainable, revise them and work diligently toward the new goals.

Players need to have something to go after, something to strive for. And it is important that what they strive for is consistent with your philosophy and objectives.

Team Goals

You can motivate an entire squad through goal setting. Try to channel your players' motives through the team. Before each season we'll discuss what we think we can realistically accomplish as a group.

Coaches who make the score their team's goal are fooling themselves. It has to be about more than that. Sure, winning X number of games can be a goal. But your chances of reaching that goal depend quite a bit on who and where you play. So winning may be impossible, even though you play as well as you can.

The goal of winning breeds inconsistent performance. Scores change all the time during a game. A team may get lazy when it is ahead or panic when it loses the lead.

So don't emphasize, "We can be 6-3 or 5-4 this season." Instead, talk about how well the team is capable of playing and then set goals for achieving that level. In years when I think we can win a conference, state, or national title, I'll be open with the players and tell them. But I'll also emphasize that they need to work hard so they don't miss their chance.

Individual Goals

Before the season I talk to each player about goals: his individual goals and his goals for the team. Each player has his own ideas. As a coach, it's important that you talk through them openly. Try to keep players' aspirations realistic and ensure that their goals are consistent with team goals.

Never tell a player that he can't achieve something, even if it is an unrealistic goal. He will have to learn sometime how to set realistic goals as a player and as a person. By learning from his mistakes about what is and is not realistic for him to do in football, maybe he'll be better able to make such judgments off the field. When you see a player getting discouraged, realizing his goals were way too high, help him adjust them appropriately.

Short-Term and Long-Term Goals

The steady, short-term target to shoot for is maximum effort, combined with good execution. A team that accomplishes this goal game in and game out will succeed.

As a long-term goal, if it is realistic, I like to aim for winning the conference. If you have a chance at being competitive against other conference teams, the conference championship becomes your long-term goal.

At the high school level, after we had achieved a consistent level of success, our goals were always

1. to be conference champion,
2. to enter the state playoffs,
3. to be state champion, and
4. to be state champion and go undefeated.

Change in Goals

Sometimes it doesn't all work out so orderly. For example, one season we lost the conference by 7 points, entered the playoffs, and won the state championship. Everybody was happy, even though all of our long-term preseason goals were not met. So we coaches decided that our future goal would be, simply, to play 13 games and win the last one.

Misdirected Goals

I never liked goals such as holding an opponent scoreless or to fewer than 100 yards rushing. Naturally, like everybody else we try to shut out each opponent for as long as we can, but I never overemphasized that to my players.

 NO SIDETRACKS

We were rolling along undefeated and unscored upon one season. During the fourth quarter of the fifth game, the opposing quarterback completed a scoring pass against what was our JV squad. An assistant said, "Oh, gosh!" I asked, "What's the matter?" He said, "Oh, they scored on us, our first touchdown given up this year." I said, "Hey, that's good." Looking surprised, he asked, "Why do you say that?" I answered, "It's good because we shouldn't try to play two games in one. If we do, the other team may score two more times before we get back on track. See, if we are chasing a meaningless goal like shutting someone out it will sidetrack us from our more important goal of going undefeated." That is why I have never emphasized such goals.

When the season is over, the only thing most fans and media care about is how many football games you won. They aren't too concerned whether you had more first downs than your opponents. And no team that set its sights on being Number 1 in first downs ever achieved long-term success, or recognition for their "accomplishment."

Be Consistent

Consistency is a trademark of winning teams. Consistent effort and performance may sound boring to some, but you couldn't trade me two All-American players for consistency in those two areas. Winning streaks are built on consistency, and they are achieved through the efforts of many, not just one or two individuals.

You are the key factor. Your team will be consistent only if you

- *emphasize playing hard* and *as a team* more than anything else,
- *provide discipline* that supports a sound philosophy, and
- *set an example* by staying on an even keel.

Emphasize Playing Hard

The overriding goal to strive for is to *give maximum effort all the time*. Consistency comes when goals are independent of the opposition's performance. To be consistent, emphasize your team's play and be less concerned about your opponent. The key is to teach players to play as hard as they can and to play together as a team. The beauty of that perspective is that players will always be motivated and not waiver according to who they are playing or whether they win or lose.

So when you talk to the team before the season don't identify any particular game as *the* game. Emphasize that each game is vitally important and worth preparing for. That's why they lift weights; that's why they run wind sprints; that's why they give their all every day in practice.

But no matter what you do, some teams underachieve. Others overachieve. Obviously, you'd rather have your team reach its potential every year. And it will if you do what you can to nurture consistency, which results from players giving maximum effort in every practice and game.

 LOSING THE EDGE

During our 52-game unbeaten streak, the 1968 team was equal in talent to its competition. We had lost two great All-State backs to graduation, and everybody felt our streak was about to end. But that year we had the most determined group of kids a coach could ever ask for. Their mental attitudes just would not let them lose. They won with scores like 21-20 and 13-7. Finally, we were tied, and I think it was because the week before we had clinched the conference title, and the players didn't play quite as hard as they could. After playing all-out to achieve the title, they seemed to play like they were almost afraid of losing.

Consistency is even more important in playoffs. You play one bad game then, and you have played your last. Playoffs teach you the value of consistency, but by the time you learn the lesson, it's usually too late.

Consistency Versus Records. Some coaches think statistical records are a great motivator. They have a back try to gain 1,000 yards rushing, and so forth.

I disagree with that approach because it places individual achievement above the team. Maybe that is why my teams have been very similar statistically every year. We shoot for having all of our backfield *positions* gain 1,000 yards. We don't identify a single running back, but rather the position. We motivate and build depth at the same time.

We have set some national records at Augustana for team offense and defense. All of those records were achieved by consistent play, *not* by emphasizing the record over the game.

 NO PASSING FANCY

We always try to be honest with players we want to recruit. I remember talking with a parent of an All-State quarterback, who in our system would be a drop-back passer, and I said, "No, we run the football first here. [Our quarterback is more of an option and running type, not a drop-back passer.] So although we would love to have you here, we don't teach your style of play." He went to another school. But the next year the quarterback who played behind him in high school came here.

We also had a young man who wanted to transfer here from Indiana. He thought that in our system he could run for all kinds of records on this level. I told him point-blank that if that's what he was thinking, he probably wouldn't be satisfied, because we emphasize the team and the game, not individual records.

How would you feel if you were on the opposite side of a team going for a single-game passing record while you are already losing 50-0? If you believe in going for such records, don't complain. But I prefer to look at the bigger picture and base our goals on more important things.

 TEAM SUCCESS = INDIVIDUAL REWARDS

Our players understand that they're more likely to receive individual awards because they're part of a successful program. For example, the first year that we were undefeated here (1981), our captain (Greg Bednar, a great player and academic All-American) turned to me after the conference awards meeting and said, "Look how many guys we got on the All-Conference Team!" He and the others saw that the system rewards individuals who are part of a successful program. That's why my office walls are covered with pictures of every All-American we've had, and yet not one ever led the country in an individual stat. In fact, we rarely have anyone on our team lead the conference in a statistical category.

Provide Discipline

You should promote the same values and teach the same way each day. In other words, don't switch from being an easy-going coach to a strict disciplinarian. That's like switching from the wishbone to the shotgun with no advance warning. All it will do is confuse and frustrate your players, and they will learn little from their experience.

Players need a predictable atmosphere in which to learn. They need assurance and confidence to put forth the kind of effort and attention required for consistent play.

Players also need to understand the value of participating on a team. We are losing kids from football because many coaches aren't making it a valuable experience for them. Our emphasis on winning has left a lot of disappointed former football players in its wake. The athletes say, "If I'm not Number 1, I'm dropping out." That's where the whole

cycle starts, down through junior high school.

Although values have changed, kids haven't changed much. They still like to have discipline and guidance, as long as it is consistently applied to the whole team.

 NO RELISH FOR THIS HOT DOG

My first year at Augustana, we had a "hot-dog" player who also was our punter. During the fourth quarter of the first game that year, we were two touchdowns ahead. We had about a 4th-and-2 situation, so we were in punt formation. But when the ball was snapped, the punter ran toward the first-down marker and made it.

I rarely scold a player in public, but this time the first thing I did, right in front of the rest of the squad, was chew out the punter for not punting as instructed. He said, "But I made it, Coach!" And I said, "I don't care if you made a touchdown, you can't operate separately from the team." The player adjusted and became All-Conference.

Parental Influences

Some players try out for the team because their parents (usually the dad) want them to. Too often, the parents' priorities are not the same as the boy's. It may be a case of a father wanting to experience things vicariously through his son.

 PARENT TRAP

One player, who played behind an All-American, had a father who couldn't understand why his boy wasn't playing more. The kid was doing a great job in practice, but he just didn't have courage on the football field. I mean, if he was running full speed at a runner who also was running full speed, this player would let up. He really looked like a player until it came to crunch time; then he just didn't have it.

I kept trying to make it clear to the father that his son wasn't starting because he had an All-American in front of him. But the dad cornered me, and finally I had to tell him the blunt truth about why his boy was on the bench. It really hurt him, but I couldn't say anything else. Believe me, I tried to say everything else that I could not to hurt his feelings, but he was so persistent that I finally just had to tell the hurtful truth.

Generally, though, parents want the best for their sons, and they trust you to provide it. Parents are a very important part of a successful program, even though some may try to influence and dominate your program.

Set an Example

Motivation is the head coach's responsibility. If after the game you tell the press, "Well, we just didn't play with any emotion and intensity," you are admitting to not having done your job in influencing attitude and mental preparation.

Coaches must work hard all the time and set an example. The players will reflect you. If you are excited and ready to go, they know it, they sense it. Conversely, if you are down or seem uninterested, they sense that and play that way.

 EMOTIONAL LOSS

I remember losing one game we could have won. The reason we lost was that I didn't bounce back from a loss the week before until about Thursday. I was feeling sorry for myself for too long, and the squad reflected my attitude.

One of the hardest things to do is come back emotionally after a loss and get your squad up. But you had better get it out of your system. Come Monday you have only five practices to get ready to play. If you waste Monday, Tuesday, Wednesday, and Thursday feeling sorry for yourself, then you have just reduced your team's chance of winning by 80%. In those situations, I say what I have to say on Monday, and it's over. That's it. I tell them, "Let's go on from here, and if you can't be 9-0 you can be 8-1."

As a head coach you have responsibilities to 50 or 100 people. If you are the leader, you have to show that you can bounce back. Kids are very perceptive; you can't fool them. If you don't bounce back, neither will they.

A Coaching Requirement: Intrinsic Motivation

I've been very fortunate to have my job as my hobby, too. I love coaching. I have found all my life that I could study football or think about it in my spare time. And it's been a source of comfort during lonely or disappointing times in my life. It helps me relax and takes my mind off problems. I am thankful that my profession is something I find such pleasure in. If it wasn't, I'd have burned out long ago.

The first source of motivation must come from within. If you are ready to go, you can inspire your players. But keep in mind that each group of players is just a little different and responds differently. The greatest motivator for high school players is to emphasize that you want them to enjoy the game. They have enough other things in their lives to be serious about.

Motivating players to concentrate and stay focused is a key to coaching. You've got to focus their attention on their individual responsibilities throughout the week and stay on a Friday-to-Friday or Saturday-to-Saturday schedule. You can't blow off days of preparation and win. They are vital. Emphasize repeatedly that players must be particularly sharp and attentive and work hard in practice.

 GOOD TUESDAY = GOOD FRIDAY

Tuesday was the big practice day for us in high school because we would like to taper off on Wednesdays, not do any hitting on Thursday, and play the game Friday. I can remember hearing one kid yelling in the locker room, "Hey, this is the last Tuesday." The players knew it was their final Tuesday practice of the year, and they were motivating themselves to have a good practice. They knew how important that practice was to their success on Friday night. They understood that the routine we had was effective. I think that helped them as they counted down to a big game.

Avoid Complacency

Complacency is the perception that good things will happen without much effort. When a team wins regularly, it's easy to let things slide. Instead of having a hard practice on Wednesday, you may have a light practice.

I've fallen into that trap, and it hurt the team. We got so good—or so we thought—that players knew the hard work was done after Wednesday. Wednesday became a party night for some, and we wound up with a two-cycle week. The players would work only on Tuesday and Wednesday and then again Saturday.

In such a situation, your discipline erodes slowly, even as you keep rolling up the victories. And instead of addressing problems as they arise, you ask yourself, "Should I blow up about this little thing? Is it worth it?" The year before you really would have laid the law down, but now you don't want to disrupt anything. And you let more and more things go.

Sometimes it takes a loss to make you reassess what you are doing and get back to the basics. You realize it's the little things that make the difference.

Never Get Self-Satisfied

I've seen good teams play at a high level early in the season, then falter. No matter how well a team plays, it's important that it raise its level of play steadily during the season. That won't happen unless your players feel they need to keep working.

In practice and in everything we do, we strive for steady improvement throughout the season. It is consistent with our philosophy of not being satisfied. We want to be the best we can be, to maximize our performance as a team and individually.

No team stays at one level. Either it will improve with effort or drop off because of lack of effort.

Not *Should*, But *Can*

I hate the word *should* in sports. I hear players and coaches all the time say, "We should have beaten them." And maybe they *could* have won the game, but one team is not predestined to beat another.

We try to teach our players never to think that something *should* happen. We say we *can* make it happen. We have to make the most of our opportunities in every practice and in every game. We have to earn our success.

Punish Rarely

I am not a punishing coach. A player can't learn football or lessons about life by running laps for punishment.

The same is true for obvious errors. A player knows when he's made a mistake. You don't cut a player's playing time unless he's made multiple errors and has failed to do his job for the rest of the team. If he has made an apparent error, there is not much you can do. He will correct it or be replaced by someone who can.

What to Punish

Punish the mental mistakes—errors in performance caused by a lack of concentration or poor communication. Remind players that successful teams make few such errors.

Because mental mistakes are so costly and demoralizing, you cannot tolerate them. If a player is so distracted that he is making critical errors in judgment, you will probably have to take him out. You can't tolerate a player blocking the wrong man or throwing to the wrong receiver. Those errors have nothing to do with ability; they demonstrate the player's lack of focus.

When you have to punish players, still treat each of them fairly. You are open to being judged unfairly by those you scold, so make sure you are fair *and* consistent.

Playing Time as a Motivator

You control your players' playing time—which is what most want more than anything else. That's your button for motivation should you need to push it.

Players should know that they are practicing to play in the game, and if they don't perform on the practice field, they won't play in the game.

Dropping players to the second team or removing them from the game is effective motivation. Call it punishment if you will. If a starter is not playing to his potential, you can't leave him in. It's really hard sometimes when you've got a big, strong, fast guy out there who's just going through the motions. But he is of no value to the team unless he is giving the effort.

 NEARLY BLEW THE CHANCE

One year, our fullback got hurt and we moved up the second-string fullback to the starting lineup. The back-up was a sophomore who usually gave us a great effort in practice. But when he moved to first string, he decided that he didn't need to block anymore. It wasn't long before we had a freshman who *was* blocking replace him as the first-string fullback. Once the sophomore realized his mistake, he worked himself back to a starting spot and never took another loafing step. As a senior he became an All-American.

Team-Oriented Discipline

Although we run a very disciplined program, I would never recommend a don't-do-this approach. Discipline must be self-motivated.

Stay focused on the big picture and don't waste time examining what each player can't do. Then, when some kind of disciplining is called for, keep things team-oriented. If you need to punish anyone, the whole team should bear the responsibility. So when one guy loafs during a conditioning drill, the whole team, not just the loafer, repeats it.

When somebody goes off-sides in a game, the whole team is penalized, not just the player who jumped. The officials don't say that only the left tackle must line up 5 yards back on the next play. The whole team goes 5 yards back. So I try to make the point, whenever possible, that everyone is responsible to the team.

So set guidelines the team as a group can commit to. Most of our life, discipline means commitments to others—family, friends, or teammates. Each player should believe the entire team depends on him.

Give Players a Say

I am pleased when a player takes the initiative to make the team stronger. He'll say, "Coach, I didn't like the way we did this or that." Or, "I didn't like the attitude of our upperclassmen." You get some good input by being receptive to their comments.

When you open the door to players' suggestions, be prepared for some negative feedback. It's natural for kids to gripe every now and then. Football is hard work, and a coach's decisions are not always easy to accept. So we sometimes say jokingly that if all the kids are happy, we must not be working them hard enough.

If a player asks why he isn't getting much playing time, be ready to answer him honestly and explain. If you can't give a player a reason, he probably *should* be playing. He may not agree with your reason, but make clear to him that you have given it thought and have evaluated the other player as better. Then encourage him to show, in future practices, that you are wrong.

Coaches get in trouble when they think they are doing everything right. Obviously we aren't. We always must try to understand the players' viewpoints and help them see why we made our decisions.

Additional Considerations About Motivation

Your approach has to be appropriate for your players' developmental stage. You coach a Little Leaguer differently than you coach a high schooler, and a high schooler differently than a college player. They play for different reasons and are sensitive to different things. A youth football player may just want to be on a team with a friend; a high schooler may play because Mom and Dad wanted him to be on the team; a college player might participate for the scholarship.

Kids rarely have just one reason for playing. It's much more complex than that, and so everyone is not turned on the same way. Try to get to know players' individual personalities and emphasize the part of your personality that best complements theirs.

Myths About Motivation

• *The team that practices the most will win the most.* Sometimes the best thing is to give players some time off. Just tell them, "Don't come to practice tomorrow; we need a day off." Sometimes you need time away as much as they do.

• *The more time together, the stronger the team unity.* Some coaches meet with kids to a fault and make getting together seem like a chore. After a while, players get nothing out of it because they are tired of all the chalk talks and of being robbed of social and study time.

• *The more hours spent in preparation, the more prepared the team.* The coaches who say, "I spent more hours in that office and film room than . . ." haven't necessarily coached any better or motivated their kids any more than coaches who spent less time in their offices. Ask yourself: How much do my players know? How much are they interested in learning from me? Are they attentive? Do they enjoy practices? Are they losing interest?

• *What works to motivate one team will work for every team.* Sometimes we fall into a pattern. What we did on August 30 last year we do again this August 30. We sometimes forget that we have 50 new players who may not respond well to what we did with last season's squad. We lost a game once because I used the charts from the year before that had worked so well without rethinking how this year's team differed from last year's. When you think you've got it all solved and there's nothing new to do, that's when you run into a problem. We were defeated handily by a team we could have beaten.

The Ultimate Motivation

Most players who stick out our program like it. They like it because they get the intangibles, and they feel they can see their growth as people in addition to their development as football players. For example, a few years ago one of our starters decided before his senior year to drop football so he could devote more time to graduate school preparation. That didn't bother me in the least. In fact, I take great pride in that because to be able to make such a positive decision for his future shows he matured a great deal during his first 3 years on the team.

Football is not forever. I never talk football as life. We never make it bigger than the first two principles (faith and family). If a player decides to leave our program to strengthen himself in another area, I'm happy because it means he's growing up a little bit.

 THE RIGHT MOTIVES

I once encouraged a starter on a national championship team to go on a European student exchange quarter the following fall, even though he could have started on our second consecutive championship team. It was a hard decision for him. He loved the game and being a part of the program, but he had plans to major in international law. Sure, I hated to lose him, but I knew that it was the right choice for his future. As a coach you must realize that football is only part of the kids' educations, and that some day soon their participation in that game is going to end.

I think our players like to play here because they get the freedom to play the game as a game. We also allow them to assume responsibility for their lives. We don't decide what classes they should take or tie up all their free time. They have to decide what to do to be successful in football and in life.

A player who can't handle that responsibility doesn't play. That's only right, because he obviously has more fundamental and important things to address before football.

Summary

1. I believe the best motivation you can give a young man is the freedom to succeed through hard work. Our players have the freedom to fail by not taking the extra step, or the chance to succeed by working hard.
2. If somebody comes along who works a little harder and takes their spot away from them, they will have at least learned something: That is the way of this competitive world, and you had better accept it because it will be that way throughout your lives.
3. Motivation that springs from a philosophy of the three Fs, hard work, self-responsibility, and personal growth will make players more successful after their football-playing days. They learn that if they work and keep working, they have a good chance of succeeding—not necessarily winning. But if they sit back and watch the other guy move ahead of them, they have already settled for second or third best.
4. As a coach, keep in mind that yours is an educational pursuit. If all you're going to give a football player is a win-loss record and a letter, you will fail.
5. You have the potential to inspire a player, through proper motivation, to develop a work ethic, a strong sense of social connectedness, and an appreciation for physical activity that will lead him to a successful and healthy future.

Chapter 4

Building a Football Program

In high school the program is the whole thing. To be a consistent winner at the high school level—maybe on any level, but especially on the high school level—you either have to "outprogram" your opponents or outnumber them.

If you are fortunate enough to coach at a school much larger than any of your opponents, you can be a consistent winner because of numbers. But that's unlikely to happen; conferences tend to attract schools of similar enrollments, interests, and locations.

Geneseo High School had about 700 kids in its four classes while I was there. It was considered a Class 3A when Illinois had five classes and moved to a 4A school when Illinois went to six classes.

People sometimes make light of the 1A champion in comparison with the 6A champion. There is no question that the 6A champion is a better football team than a 1A champion. Nobody argues that. But it is just as hard to be a champion in 1A as it is in 6A.

So the coach of the 1A state champion has accomplished just as much as the coach of a 6A champion. That's why the program is the key to success at each level. You must have a better system, better staff, and better prepared players than the other coaches in your school's classification.

Initiating a Program

In most high schools, you can't recruit players to fill positions. You have to take what's there. You must get the most out of the players available to you. You must not only develop them physically for your style of play, but also adapt them mentally to your philosophy.

Selecting a Style

To start, you must determine how you want your players to play the game. You may choose to be a ball-control, running team or to be a wide-open, passing football team. Don't get too complex or you'll confuse the players, if not yourself. Select a system flexible enough that you can feature the talent you have each year without changing the fundamentals taught through your program.

You must believe absolutely in the system of play you choose. That's the only way you can sell it and teach it to players. If you doubt the system, the players will reflect that in a lack of acceptance and poor performance.

Generating Interest

To create interest in the program, sell it to the players. You recruit by encouraging. You go to the junior high school and sell yourself and your program. Let the young people see that you are interested in them and the school.

You may have to recruit at the high school too, especially if you are a new coach and the program has been down a bit. You will need to create some interest among kids in the school who could help you by playing.

But, remember, your first responsibility is to players who have already committed themselves to the program. If they believe in you, they will sell their friends.

  CREDIT WHERE CREDIT'S DUE

When I first went to Geneseo High School, it had won one game in 2 years. We had 16 varsity football players. All sophomore games the year before were forfeited because there weren't enough players. The first school assembly was bad—everybody was criticizing and making fun of the athletes.

So after I introduced the players (all 16 of them), I scolded the rest of the students at the assembly. I turned to my team and said to them, "Whenever you hear these people, these talkers and not doers, say to you that you are no good, remember this: This is *your* football team. If anybody up there says he's better, he's lying because he doesn't have the courage even to try." Then I asked the students to treat the players with respect, and to remember this: "The players before you are the best football team that this school can produce for this season. These players have a right to be proud. And you, the student body, should back them, win or lose!"

I did this because I wanted to pat the players on the back and let them know I felt they were important to me and the program's future. I wanted them to know the program would do fine with them as our representatives, and that I had confidence in them.

Teaching the System

Once you choose your style of play and generate enthusiasm for it, do all you can to teach it. Say that you have decided to use an "odd" defensive front. Then, within that alignment, you determined whether you are going to have players sit-watch-read or try to pressure. Keep in mind that whatever defensive options you select, they won't do you any good if you don't teach them effectively.

Teach the same, sound fundamentals and philosophy of the system to players at all levels. Then, younger players will develop with the skills and attitude they need to succeed when they reach the varsity level. And, over several years of learning, they'll master that style; perhaps as important, they'll develop a strong belief in it.

Initially, the style you put into a program may cost you some victories at lower levels. But as younger players learn and develop the skills you emphasize, the wins will come. By the time your freshmen are seniors, they should demonstrate total understanding of your program.

Just as importantly, grade schoolers will develop an attitude and begin working to play varsity. They will have heroes on the team, and that identification will motivate them to work and improve.

The program, then, almost automatically restocks itself with well-disciplined and motivated players. When the program reaches a consistently high performance level for several years, you'll know it has arrived.

Developing Players

Because most of your players won't be another Joe Montana, Jim Brown, or Dick Butkus, you'll have to develop available talent. But keep in mind their level of development. You can't coach a seventh grader the same way you coach a varsity player.

At the lower level, emphasize participation to keep players involved. Normal attrition of players from junior high to high school means you'll need a large pool of seventh and eighth graders if you expect good turnouts for the freshman and sophomore teams. That's tough because young people have so many other things to do besides play football. You have to make it more worthwhile for them than simply standing on the sidelines watching their peers play. They can do that from the stands, *and* talk to their girlfriends at the same time.

I am often surprised at how a seemingly hopeless case at the seventh-grade level can turn into an all-conference performer by senior year. Conversely, sometimes a boy who has matured a little faster than others might be a Little League superstar, but by the time he's a senior may be lagging.

      DIAMONDS IN THE ROUGH

When I went to Geneseo, I was the fresh-soph basketball coach. I strongly believe that at the fresh-soph level you should play a lot of kids. Out of 15 players, 10 or 11 of them were real close in ability. So I asked the head varsity coach what he thought about me platooning them, substituting in groups of five so all would get approximately equal playing time.

The win-loss record was not that important to me. I thought it was more important for each player to get a chance to develop at that level. The head coach told me to do as I wished. I platooned all year and still had a winning season.

By the time that group became seniors it was a good team. But two who had started were no longer part of the team, and two who were part of the second-platoon team ended up being all-conference players. They were late developers.

That taught me something. Before then, I had given most of the playing time to what I believed was the first team. If I had continued that, the second stringers wouldn't have played nearly as much or developed as well as they did.

Promoting Participation

Some of the best high school sports programs have four or five junior highs feeding them. No question, part of their success is sheer numbers. But the real key is that the kids coming into the program have all had an opportunity to play.

Junior High Level. When I started the high school football program in Geneseo, I split the players at one junior high school into two equal teams. This was the only way to get all of them more playing time. We went from being limited to no more than 22 starters to having as many as 44 starters!

We avoided designating a "first" group and a "second" group. I didn't want to identify the best players at that level. The kids know who the best players are anyway; you don't have to say the green team is better than the white team.

The varsity coaching staff didn't pick the two junior high teams. Instead, the two teams' coaches would pick the players, as in the pro draft. They would try to fill all positions and try to balance the teams' talent. They did a good job of choosing up fair sides. The teams played the same schedule, including a game against each other, which was usually close because the teams were so even. The teams also practiced together and would scrimmage each other once in a while.

The next step is to attend as many lower-level games as possible. When I was building the program, I went to almost every game at the lower levels. Even after the program was established, I tried to see as many games as I could. The head coach must show the young people participating in the program he is interested in them.

Attending these games also lets you observe the coaches in your program and see if your philosophy is being followed.

Freshman-Sophomore Level. You start to lose a few players from the program when they become freshmen and sophomores. Those who do come out are interested in playing, so you can get more involved in teaching techniques and perhaps become more demanding of the players.

The freshman-sophomore level is a great place for a coach to start emphasizing little things that make the program special. And you can apply more of the philosophy and discipline behind the program. For example, if a player steps out of line in the classroom, the coach might make the player sit out a game. It teaches the player that more is expected at that level and that he'll have to decide whether his desire to play is strong enough to adhere to the program's discipline and values.

It's better for a coach to teach values at early stages in the player's development than at the varsity (junior-senior) level. First, winning becomes a bigger issue to people around the program as the player advances to varsity. The player better have his priorities in order or he'll succumb to the pressure. Second, the athlete must maintain high academic standards to be eligible for a college athletic scholarship. Third, the varsity coach should not have to worry about discipline if training at lower levels is adequate.

To maximize participation, we created a freshman team and a sophomore team. We allowed the best freshmen to play on the sophomore team, but freshmen could not play on both teams. It doesn't do a kid any good to play 20 games against lesser competition. We also created a junior varsity schedule for the same purpose: to allow for maximum and appropriate competitive participation. These schedules allow a coach to promise every boy in the program an opportunity to play every week.

Building Depth

Building depth is the hardest thing to do when you're building a program. Coaches often feel they have to stay close in games they have no chance to win. So instead of substituting younger guys who can help the team next year, the coach leaves the veterans in because he thinks they'll keep the score "respectable."

It's important to build depth at lower levels and wait for those kids to mature. If all players know the fundamentals and work together, winning will take care of itself. Some coaches believe in instant success, but there is no such thing. You've got to lay a foundation, then build on that foundation.

Getting Administration Support

On-the-field instruction is critical, but a lot of the building process happens off the gridiron. School administrators' decisions will have a significant impact on your ability to get the football program going and to keep it going.

Your team will need well-maintained facilities, good equipment, qualified medical staff and supplies, and adequate uniforms. I always tell my school's administrators that I don't need more of those items than an opposing school's football team has, but it can't be done with less.

If the opposition has 8 assistant coaches, then get 8. Don't accept 5, and don't ask for 10. You should never be asked to build a program with fewer basic resources than the opposition. Small schools can't outnumber their opponents, so they need quality facilities and equipment or they will be at a distinct disadvantage.

Most administrators will support your requests if they are well-conceived and reasonable.

Gaining Community Support

If you coach at a community school, you've got to make your program part of that community *and* tie it closely to other school activities. Some coaches make a mistake in separating the football program and its revenue from the rest of the school.

Your program should be a part of the educational system and be the school administration and school board's responsibility. They must provide the funds for that program. You should fulfill the needs of the program within the budget set aside. I'm not talking about frills here, just necessities.

A good booster group is like having another team. It can help sell your program and bring the community together. This is particularly true in a larger school, where booster club meetings allow strangers to interact. The boosters may never see each other outside the meetings because they go to different churches, different stores, and live several miles apart.

In a smaller community, almost everyone knows one another and sees each other almost daily. They share the same bank, grocery store, and post office. Whether your program is big or small, it's helpful to have a strong booster club that provides a unifying influence and financial support.

Boosters should never provide basic equipment for the program. That's the responsibility of the school board. To me the key word is *need*. The school is responsible for meeting your needs (helmets, shoulder pads, practice field, etc.). If you want an extra frill, like a fancy blocking sled in addition to your basic one, then maybe boosters or a local business can help.

You want the school to be in control of your finances. If you continually go to the boosters, they will come to control you (meaning they will hold the power to hire and fire). That isn't what you want. You want your job in the hands of the school administration.

The Private School Advantage

Private schools have an ideal situation for coaches to teach the important values of sport. And they also have an advantage, particularly in cities, when it comes to building a program because private school coaches can recruit from other districts. Privately funded schools also typically have many social events that bring people together—spaghetti suppers, raffles, and whatever else it takes to keep the school running. Parents of players, other families in the school, and boosters get to know each other through the

events they attend together, and everyone is working for the school and for the athletic teams. That helps strengthen school unity and team support.

We built a public high school program as if it were in a private school. We called the football program a community project so everybody could share in it. And that's what happened. The youth football program (Grades 5–7) was run by the community entirely. (The eighth grade through varsity program was run by our school system.) Everyone involved could take pride in helping the program, and they felt closer to the players because they had a hand in their development. That's one advantage smaller communities enjoy: People more readily identify with the individual players. They aren't just anonymous kids in football gear; the fans really want to help them.

 WHAT GOES AROUND . . .

Scouts sometimes give us fuel for motivation. One time a couple Chicago-area scouts came down to watch us. Our farm community was quite a shock to them. And they apparently found our town and our team not to be very impressive. They sat up in the stands with all of our fans, talking about how superior their team was to ours. They pointed out one player in particular: "41 out there looks like the weak sister."

Well, that happened to be our guard, Bob Orsi, who later became a high school All-American and played 4 years at the University of Missouri. Knowing Bob's temperament, we would poke fun at him during the whole week before a game with the scout's words: "Hey, weak sister Bob!" When we finally played against that Chicago-area school, Bob caused four fumbles on his first four tackles. He played with incredible enthusiasm, no doubt spurred by the scouts' unfavorable assessment.

Coaching Staff Development

You can't start a football program alone. You need the assistance of a strong staff. They must believe that you have a method that will succeed and that you know it inside and out. You must be willing to delegate responsibilities to them, then adjust their duties depending on their ability to fulfill them.

Sometimes you may reassign a coach because his personality is not right for a certain level of athlete. Some of the best seventh- and eighth-grade coaches are people who just can't be good varsity coaches and vice versa. You may inherit assistants you probably wouldn't have selected. They are proof of why the program hasn't been successful. Some may be coaching for a $400 differential. Others may just want to be called "Coach."

When assistant coaches fail to fulfill their duties, you must take away their responsibility. And that means you'll probably have to assume some of those duties yourself until you can make a change. But you have to make a change. Coaches, like players, must be sold on the program philosophy if they are going to be helpful.

Keeping Staff Members Equal

I was always adamant that my high school assistant coaches be paid the same. That let me organize my staff to best help our program without worrying that I was denying someone's family an income.

Because the assistants knew they got equal pay, they always had great camaraderie. When all coaches are at the same salary, no one of them feels he's any more or less than any other member of the staff.

I have never believed in "I'm just the freshman coach" or "I'm just the assistant junior high coach." There is no *just* anything. If you're good and you contribute to the program, you shouldn't have to qualify your role. I think the coaches on my staffs have felt very much a part of whatever success we enjoyed because I gave them the opportunity to coach and didn't interfere.

Giving Staff Authority

At all coaching levels, you must let your coaches coach. I never tried to dictate exactly what defense or offense they should run. However, I did insist that all of our coaches run the varsity's basic style. In other words, they numbered their offensive plays as we did and had the same basic core of plays.

 A LITTLE RAZZLE DAZZLE

I remember sitting in the press box of a freshman game when one of our coaches called some super-duper end-around pass. Well, everyone in the press box looked to see my reaction. And I just shrugged my shoulders and said, "He didn't

get that play from me. I don't have one of those in our playbook. In fact, I have never *seen* it before."

I wasn't unhappy that the freshmen were running a play like that. I thought it was good they were learning a few new wrinkles and that the coach was exercising the freedom that I encourage. Coaches need the flexibility to work with their teams in their style. Still, too much variation too often should not be allowed.

You can't just give a coach the freshman team and then never talk with him. You have to familiarize all the coaches in the program with your approach and let them get comfortable with it. Soon it will be automatic for them.

United You Stand, Divided You . . .

It's vital that your staff work well together. That will, to no small degree, determine how well your players work together. If one assistant is critical of other assistants, your players are likely to be divided in their feelings toward the coaches. It's similar to when a father scolds a son but then the boy gets pacified by the mother.

If your coaches cooperate and believe in your philosophy, you're going to function smoothly as a staff. If the coaches are truly together, the players will sense it and perform as a team.

A football staff, in some ways, demands a military command hierarchy. You have 25 seconds to make a decision. And just as there is no right or wrong way to play the game, there may be no right or wrong deci-

sion. But the sure way to fail is when half of the staff think it's right and the other half think it's wrong. It's the same in war. There may be no right or wrong way to take the hill, but if half go one way and half go the other way, you are not going to take the hill. The same is true in football; time does not allow for second-guessing the head coach.

Key Points to Initiating a Program

- Choose and study a system of play.
- Sell your players on that style of play.
- Teach the system of play soundly and repeatedly.
- Build a feeder system at the lower levels that maximizes participation and institutes your style of play throughout.
- Get the necessary support of the school administration and the community.
- Develop a strong coaching staff that is united and competent.

Turning a Program Around

We were fortunate to win four games during my first year at Geneseo, when realistically we had hoped to win one or two. We won six games each of the next two seasons. The fourth season we were 25 seconds from going undefeated and finished 8-1. After that we didn't lose again for 6 years. The program was well established by the fourth season, but it continued to develop steadily over the next decade.

If you ever go undefeated your first year at a school, you have to give credit to the guy ahead of you. He did a great job, whether he won or lost, in getting the talent prepared in the early years. And you may be all that the program needed to change the players' attitude.

The first year is very important. Expectations are high and everyone treats you great. So the first year, realistic goals are most important. Make the attitude more positive and get players to play hard throughout each game. You don't necessarily need a great winning record, but people must see that the players are enjoying football and that you're moving in the right direction.

Instilling a Winning Attitude

I soon realized that all the ideas I had on building a program were not worth a nickel if we weren't successful on the varsity level. You can have a great philosophy, but if it doesn't work, you're gone.

When you are in a complete losing situation at the varsity level, you may need to do things to win a little more on the lower level to build confidence. Teams begin to expect either to win or to lose after a while. You want your players to think positively.

All for One

Everyone in the program needs the same objectives, because you'll succeed as a group. Each season the general objective is to be as good as you can be. If that objective is the same for the coach and for the team, both will be equally responsible for preparing for practice each day.

The cliche is that "it takes character to win." That shouldn't be why a coach teaches character. You should teach your team to play hard for four quarters of every game, not to quit in any situation, and to do all it can to help each member play better. Help players learn to work with other people and to sacrifice for others and for themselves. Those are the lessons.

When you see a score of 85-0, it means one team was far superior to the other. But it also may be the case that the other team gave up; it just didn't care anymore. The real difference between the teams may be around 40 points, not 85. So the coach of the losing team owes it to his players to teach them that if an opponent is 40 points better, make sure it beats you only by 40 points. That's a lesson: Never give up.

Base your program on a philosophy (chapter 1) in which winning isn't the only objective. Here's a sample philosophy that doesn't make light of the importance of winning but recognizes that football is about much more than that: Participate to win, but judge your success on whether you were as good as you can be. Or, to paraphrase scripture, "Run the race so as to win."

Teamwork is the first test of your program. You'll know you are on your way when players demonstrate their belief in what you are doing. When you see them start to execute the fundamentals you are teaching, along with the teamwork and unity, you'll find that the winning will take care of itself.

Getting That Effort

The first step in creating a winning environment is to see that all players play hard. Emphasize this at your first meeting: "Play four quarters, and if you are getting beat by 15 points, make sure you don't get beat by 30. Play until your last ounce of energy is used up; that's the way you get better."

If you take this approach, your team will win a game or two by the end of the year, just because your kids keep giving it their all. But in addition to another victory or two, playing full speed is important because

- it's the only way players will improve (and therefore the only way the team will improve), and
- players will be less likely to get hurt.

Players in the losing habit sometimes give up in the first quarter. They go into the game thinking they can't win, they get a couple of touchdowns behind, and they say, "Here we go again." Before they know it, the other team has scored two more times.

Players will be more willing to give maximum effort if they are confident in what they are doing. You can instill this attitude by establishing a way to play and by teaching that way effectively to players. When you are assured in your approach, players pick up on your confidence and feel more convinced and committed to the cause.

Acknowledge a good block or a good "read" to let players know they are coming along and that you noticed it. This convinces them the system is good and increases their effort and persistence in making it work.

Coach to the players. Reinforce them. Let them know they are important. Build them up honestly. Talk with them individually.

Discipline on the football field is much like discipline in the classroom. If you lose discipline in your classroom, you can't get it back. If you start out saying, "These are the rules, and you will live by them," you have a chance to conduct a well-organized class.

I've never agreed with compromising my principles—even when I had only 16 players on the squad. Players need guidelines, and they need to know that those rules apply to everyone.

It's crucial, first, to determine what is most important to teach your players and, then, to teach them. This is so whether you have 16 guys or 60 guys. If you get down to 14 players, don't start rationalizing that you don't have enough to play; go with what you've got and be grateful for their confidence in you.

We had a great program not just because our juniors and seniors were fundamentally sound in skills. Just as important, we knew their character was sound. Our sophomore and freshmen coaches were teaching the same philosophy as our varsity coaches.

Setting Training Rules

I have always maintained the same training rules:

- Obey the law.
- Act like a gentleman.

Those rules are all-encompassing. At both the high school and collegiate levels, players must realize they are representing more than just themselves on the field. They are also representing their school. Anyone who runs into trouble with the law will not be a football player. A player unable to conduct himself as a gentleman off the field is not ready to conduct himself as a member of the team on the field.

Players in successful programs have high visibility. If one player out of 100 makes a mistake, you can be sure the media will spotlight him. That he is a football player will reflect on the whole team.

Our two training rules are important to living a successful life. Both guidelines are general, so you have to give players specific examples to let them know what is and isn't acceptable.

For instance, a smoker would not be part of our high school football team. First, it's illegal for anyone under 17, plus it violates the health behaviors I believe are essential to being a gentleman and an athlete. As a college coach, I have no restriction against smoking, although I won't permit it in the locker room or anywhere around the football program. I can't control what a kid does in his room. I do ask players not to frequent bars, because they represent something bigger than themselves.

I also expect our players to be neat and well groomed. I tell them that although our nickname is the Vikings, we are not going to look like the Vikings from long ago. So there won't be any beards. If we go into a hotel on the road, I want anyone who sees our team to have a positive impression of Augustana football. We represent our school and our program, and our players must understand that.

During the off-season, some players grow beards, mostly to experiment with a different look. I can't control their lives. They have to be free to experiment, just as we did. Still, we try to stay aware of players' off-season activities. Their responsibilities to the program and the school don't end at the buzzer of the last game of the season.

Developing Team Pride

The best way to develop pride is to make players feel positive about being on the squad. Pat players on the back and tell them they are doing a good job. Everybody likes to be praised.

But don't forget that discipline and character come from being bumped around a little bit, from making mistakes. A wise person learns from others' mistakes and his own. A fool learns only from his own mistakes. Some players have to blunder to correct themselves, no matter how well you inform them. When players go through this error-making and correcting, keep working with them: Let them know you are a team, and that you are with them all the time.

You can't build pride by pointing the finger at them or putting them down. From chapter 1, remember that the players don't play for you. They are—and should be—playing for themselves and each other. In fact, if you think about it, you're responsible to them more than they are responsible to you.

Outstanding programs have unity—pride and faith in each other to work together. It takes at least 2 or 3 years to get everyone thinking your way, then another year or 2 before the players perform in the system as you would like.

Creating a Team Identity

Little things, such as a team ritual, can make your players feel even more special— different than players in other programs. That's why we have different-colored uniforms, or wear black or white shoes. Such rituals can help unify a team.

We do something to give each year's team its own identity. Maybe we change the color of game socks or get special practice jerseys.

I never allow our game jerseys to be sold to the public. Instead, after our seniors have worn them for 4 years, we give them to the players as keepsakes. Fans can buy similar shirts in the bookstore, but only a 4-year player gets a game jersey of his own. They are special, and I want all the players to realize that.

  THE VICTORY BELL

When an old school in town was torn down, somebody suggested salvaging the big bell in the building and putting it by the football field. Then, after each varsity home game that we won, the players could ring it to signal victory. Only the varsity could join in this special postgame activity, and it became a ritual.

I didn't realize it so antagonized the opposition. I never intended for the ringing of the victory bell to come off as if we were rubbing people's noses in it. I never thought of it that way. Yet our opponents' coaches and fans seemed to think we were being pompous.

It was intended to make being a varsity player more special. And the kids thought it was great—after they congratulated the opposing team on their effort—to run for the victory bell. Plus, the big bell had historic significance to the community because people who went to the school had fond memories of it. This became a way for them to take pride both in their past and in the present school's football program.

Starting a Tradition

If you ever saw the great Virgil Fletcher's Collinsville (Illinois) high school basketball teams play, you knew what to expect. He had a program that was built on a certain style. Every one of his teams would halfcourt press, rarely if ever use a bounce pass, and always took high-percentage shots.

If you have a great program in high school, even when you don't have great material, you should stay above 500. Then when you get the material, you can go to the top. It's difficult to go from last to first, no matter what kind of material you have. The key is to be consistently strong.

The definition of a great program is not to win every game every year. The definition of a great program is this: *Any time an opponent steps on your field, they know they will have to play their best or they will lose.* When you get a program established, teams can't overlook you. They know it, and your players know it. Even if you play below your ability, you still might win. That's tradition.

Maintaining a Program

I sometimes feel it is harder to maintain a program than to build it. In building a program, all little successes are big successes. If I am 0-9 one year but win the first game the next year, that is a great thrill for everybody. Everyplace the players go, they get patted on the back. "Hey, that's great; you guys just won one. You are going to be okay, aren't you?"

Or, if the team has been below .500 for years and it goes 6-3, that's a big deal to people. It's another progression in building the program. People around you sense it. They become excited about it, and you and the players do too.

Later, when the program is a consistent winner, everybody is on the bandwagon. Suddenly, the victories don't mean as much. Or perhaps you win but not by very much, and people get upset. The players begin hearing negative things. And even if you get a winning streak going, people don't appreciate it. Their attitude is "this is easy."

As I warned in chapter 3, complacency can be a big problem when everyone tells players how good they are and how nobody can beat them. At the same time, everyone starts thinking that the opposition is no good, that it doesn't stand a chance. Players hear all of this, and it hurts their mental edge. As a coach, monitor this and perhaps push them a little harder.

On Being King of the Hill

Other schools gang up on the perennial champion. If you are ranked Number 1 year after year, and particularly if you have a long winning streak going, it's a great feather in an opponent's cap to upset you. That brings instant notoriety to the opponent's program.

Coaches from opposing schools may share scouting information they think will help defeat you. Fans and the media are always looking for you to be upset. And officials sometimes get swept up into looking more closely for penalties against your team.

But the team on top has one advantage: The dominance you have maintained over other teams may have given your program a mystique. If you play at a high school that has never in your memory beaten your school, it is hard for the underdog to believe it can win.

In maintaining a program, the coach and the team have to be ready to accept less praise for accomplishing the same things they were lauded for in previous years. In our situation, people said we had a bad year when we lost a regular season game and didn't win the conference title. They forgot that nobody before us had ever won the conference eight times in a row. And they also thought we had a bad year in 1987 when we finally did not win a national championship after winning four straight and a record 60 consecutive games. So a coach of a strong program must realize that expectations escalate after years of winning.

Adults can live with such expectations. But it is wrong for players who have worked so hard and accomplished all they could to be criticized because of the totals on the scoreboard.

Coaches who want only to build and not

to maintain programs are either unwilling or unable to put up with such high expectations, diminishing praise, and constant pressure. Building is more exciting than maintaining. Sometimes it's hard because you love the joy and excitement associated with overcoming the odds—defeating a favored opponent. That kind of elation no longer exists when you are the favorite.

 IT ISN'T ALL LUCK

During our 60-game winning streak, we had several close games. And after those games it was funny that writers would say how lucky we were. But when I was asked about how we maintained the streak, I never used the word *lucky*. In my opinion we were simply prepared to meet each opportunity we had for 60 straight games. That's what it takes to maintain a program at a high level: extra hard preparation. Other schools we played had all the emotion on their side. For us it was just another game to win along the way. For them, beating us was the goal of their season, and perhaps careers.

Building to Another Level

The fundamental values associated with teaching football and keeping it a game have worked for me at both the high school and college levels.

I'll probably never have the opportunity to coach at a higher level, like Division I. But that's a challenge any coach who is competitive would want. It's refreshing and reinforcing to be able to visit, for example, Penn State, and see that things you believe in are done. The emphasis on education and the attitudes and actions of players are emphasized, yet the program is still very successful.

Coaches must remember that the program carries the school's name, not the coach's. It's the Augustana football team whether I'm here or not. The head coach always gets the credit for success, but in many ways that's wrong because success also takes the assistant coaches' efforts and the team's cooperation.

When I was inducted into the Quad-City Hall of Fame along with former basketball great Don Nelson and football All-Pro running back Roger Craig, I said, "The truth is that I'm different than these two people because they got in on their ability, and I got in on other people's ability."

Never fail to realize that your successes are because of so many other people. No one can do it alone. And, come to think of it, nothing you can do in life is much fun if you do it alone. What makes it fun is when you can share it with your family, your team, and the fans. So share the successes. You'll enjoy them more, and you'll have more people supporting you when a setback occurs.

Selecting A Program Builder

I am writing this closing note to all of those impatient school board members and administrators, booster club members, and fans who want a successful football program to support. My advice is to look for a coach who has these qualities:

- A well-defined philosophy consistent with the school's mission
- An ability to communicate with and teach the level of athletes he will coach
- A detailed plan for how he will implement the program
- Evidence of training in physical education and coaching-related subject matter
- Several solid references who attest to the individual's character, ability to work with student-athletes, and proper application of coaching principles and football skills and strategies

If all candidates are equal, *then* evaluate such things as years of experience, size of schools that the coach had worked for, and win-loss record. Intangibles, such as whether the coach will be satisfied with the position for a number of years, also must be considered.

A coach should be granted at least 3 years to get things turned around. If you want instant success, you are encouraging cheating. Let the coach lay a solid foundation then build from it. That's the only way to develop a football program that you, the school, and the community can take pride in.

Summary

Building a highly successful football program is a significant achievement, no matter what level of play. Here are the keys to doing so:

1. Choose a style of play that you know thouroughly, can teach well, and is flexible enough to adjust to the talents of your players and the tactics of the opposition.
2. Develop the interest and skills of players in the program and of those who will be entering it; depth is essential.
3. Seek administrative support and community backing for necessary resources and for enthusiasm.
4. Create a strong coaching staff with assistants who are treated equally and have authority to make decisions.
5. Get players to think positively, believe in your system of play, and play hard.
6. Everyone in the program must have the same objectives and live by the same set of rules.
7. Team pride and team identity won't just happen; develop them through conducting your program the right way for many years.
8. Always remember that the success of a football program requires the combined efforts of many; don't pretend or try to do it alone.

Part II
Coaching Plans

Chapter 5

Planning for the Season

Everything I talked about in Part I has an impact on the specific functions we perform as football coaches. That's why it's titled Coaching Foundation.

This section focuses on written plans essential for organized and successful coaching. Although not as much fun as drawing up Xs and Os, these plans are just as important to your program's organization and success.

In this chapter, I'll explain how we manage the details involved in planning a season. Among the most important things you'll be responsible for planning are

- equipment,
- medical services,
- physical preparation,
- scheduling,
- travel,
- staff planning, and
- player recruitment.

Equipment

You cannot ask a young man to get on a football field and collide with another player at full speed unless you equip him properly. Along with hockey players, football players require the most protective equipment of any athletes.

Some coaches emphasize the cosmetic parts of the uniform—the colors and style of the jersey, pants, and helmet. And there is something to be said for looking good and feeling proud while wearing the school colors. But most important is the quality of the pads under the shirt and pants and of the helmet on the head.

 **A FRESHMAN WHO WASN'T GREEN**

Because we had such a high player turnout, my first year at Augustana, we didn't have enough helmets that fit. I knew that the high school where I coached the year before had more than enough helmets, so we borrowed an ample supply to outfit everyone for the season. The only problem was that the high school's helmets were green. Augustana's were gold.

After an early scrimmage, some of our coaches asked, "Who's that kid in the green hat?" What caught their attention, in addition to his great play at linebacker, was his green helmet—indicating he was a freshman. That freshman in the green helmet ended up starting all four years for us, and in 1982 he became an All-American.

Start by checking the condition of leftover equipment. Get the pads and helmets cleaned and reconditioned, and check with an equipment certifier to make sure that every item meets an acceptable standard.

Helmets and shoulder pads are the key. Make sure of their quality and fit. Other protective gear such as girdle pads, thigh pads, and knee pads also must be adequate.

We learned in the infantry that a soldier is no good with sore feet, and the same is true for a football player. Get good shoes and see that players pay attention to minor foot problems.

In addition to equipment your players wear, you'll need new footballs and perhaps new blocking dummies. Plan on allocating a percentage of your annual budget to new equipment. Once you build the equipment supply to a high standard, the cost each year should remain fairly constant.

    GEAR UP FOR GAMES

When I came to Augustana, we needed to upgrade our football equipment, but our budget didn't give us much of a chance to do it. So I proposed to our president that we change our schedule.

The proposal was to drop our early-season opener. With the money we saved, we could purchase all the equipment I felt was necessary to upgrade the program. Because the cost to the college was the same, the president agreed, and we were able to meet our needs.

Some school districts have tight budgets. But liability concerns associated with foot-ball programs will force those who control the dollars to listen. If they won't give your program the funds to cover necessities, you may have to reconsider your future at the school.

Medical Services

Because football is such a hard-hitting, collision sport played by athletes who have strength and speed, a helmet and pads cannot prevent every injury. Therefore, in addition to providing good equipment, you must take another important preseason safety measure: setting up medical services your players should receive.

To make smart decisions about your program's medical needs, I recommend getting some training. You are not going to become a medical expert, but the American Coaching Effectiveness Program has a basic Sport First Aid course that provides solid information for any coach. I also urge you to get certified in CPR through the American Red Cross or the American Heart Association.

Preseason Screening and Exams

Sports medicine has come a long way from when I started coaching. I hate to think about how many injuries could have been avoided if we had known then what we know now about athletes' anatomy and physiology.

A good way to prevent injuries is to have your athletes screened medically before preseason conditioning. This screening can warn you of major health problems and detect performance-related problems, such as strength deficits and poor flexibility.

Besides this screening process—which can be performed by a certified athletic trainer or by other qualified sports medicine specialists—each player should see a physician for a complete preseason medical exam. School insurance policies often require medical clearance. Plus, it gives you and the players peace of mind to start the season.

Sports Medicine Personnel

The contrast between coaching in high school without an athletic trainer and in college where we not only have an athletic trainer but a whole staff of student trainers, makes it clear to me that every football program should be serviced by a full-time athletic trainer. A trainer's expertise leads to better physical preparation of players and offers invaluable emergency care when an injury occurs. Given the recordkeeping, insurance, and liability concerns surrounding football, I feel that every school should be mandated to hire at least one certified athletic trainer.

A team physician also should be available to players, both during games and throughout the season. Your conference or state association should have a rule that requires the host team to provide a physician on-site at every contest.

 SIDELINE CALL BY MD

During a high school playoff game in the late 1970s one of our top players had his "bell rung." He was stung pretty good and needed some help off the field.

Ordinarily I would not allow a player in that condition to return. But in this case, the player's family doctor, who was at the game, examined him and determined that he was OK to play. The player returned to the game and experienced no further problems.

Most schools are fortunate to have a sports-minded local physician interested in helping the school. If you have such a team physician, coordinate schedules to ensure that the doctor can attend games and be available at other times to examine injured players.

Both the team physician and athletic trainer can be invaluable in rehabilitating injured players. Consult these qualified sports medical specialists before allowing any injured player to return to action.

Medical Supplies

Use the expertise of your sports medicine staff to determine what medical supplies you'll need. You must not jeopardize players' well-being by trying to do without such essentials as tape, sterile gauze, and wraps. More than a liability issue, it's a priority issue, reflecting your concern that your players' health and safety not be compromised.

Physical Preparation

The days of players playing their way into condition are long past. In fact, it seems that the days of players practicing their way into condition are over too. Because of the limited number of practices possible before the first game, you cannot afford to take up much practice time on conditioning. There is so much to teach in so little time.

I've never instituted a mandatory off-season conditioning program. Instead, I have always believed that if you make being a member of the football team special, players will do what is necessary to be in shape when the season rolls around. The most significant contribution of off-season training is reducing the number of player injuries.

 ON TRACK FOR NEXT SEASON

In high school I had the advantage of also being head track coach. That allowed me to work with all the boys in a sport that really complemented football.

Even athletes who weren't real competitive runners in meets came out for track. They saw it as a way to have a good training routine for football set up for them. Plus, they liked being part of the team with their friends.

I think a coach is responsible for providing players the necessary information and tools they need to train effectively. We have always sent running programs (below) to our players during the summer to encourage them to prepare their bodies for the season.

We also give players who show an interest an off-season weight-training program suited to their needs, and we make sure they have access to the weight room. A good reference for setting up strength and conditioning programs is *Strength Training for Football* (1992), available through Human Kinetics Publishers.

Scheduling

Every head coach needs input with the athletic director to set up the season's schedule. After all, it's the head coach's job that often is in the balance and that depends on the season's results. The most important thing is to schedule competitive opponents.

Competitive Scheduling

If your conference affiliation is appropriate, you should automatically face several

---

Augustana Summer Running Program

Three running styles are used in this program. Form and distance running are emphasized initially to develop technique and endurance. Interval running is incorporated later to develop speed and explosiveness.

Form Running

1. Run in place, bringing your knees high. Accelerate slowly and run for 25 yards, emphasizing knee lift.
2. Run for 25 yards and emphasize stride length. Bring your knees high, extend your lower leg, land, and push off with the ball of your foot.
3. Run a 25-yard "goose step," keeping your weight back in drum-major fashion. You should feel the stretch in your thighs.
4. Run in place as fast as you can for 10 seconds, bringing your thighs parallel to the ground and keeping your toes pointed straight ahead.

Distance Running

Develop an endurance base early in the summer by running distances. A good average is 2 to 3 miles per workout at an 8-minutes-per-mile pace. This program places a greater emphasis on interval training because you are approaching preseason practice. Nevertheless, you should continue running distances twice a week on lifting days. End your workout with stretching exercises.

Interval Running

There are approximately 100 to 150 all-out efforts against resistance during a practice session or a game. These explosive efforts last 5 to 15 seconds and require an enormous expenditure of energy. The recovery time between efforts is usually a period of active rest (for example, when a receiver jogs back to the huddle). Thus, you can see that interval training is a necessary part of preparing for preseason practice. You should perform all your workouts using maximum effort. The rest:work ratio should be 3:1 for distances of 100 yards or less. For example, if you run an 11.0 hundred, you should rest 33 seconds. The rest interval for distances of 110 to 140 yards is 2:1; for distances greater than 440 it is 1:1. Current research has indicated that the rest period should consist of walking or jogging.

The following program consists of 2 to 3 miles of intervals per workout. Each week add one repetition to the following distances: 60, 40, and 20 yards.

First week

Jog 880
Run 880, rest is 1:1
Run 2 440s, rest is 2:1
Run 2 220s, rest is 2:1
Run 2 100s, rest is 3:1
Run 2 60s, rest is 3:1
Run 2 40s, rest is 3:1
Run 2 20s, rest is 3:1

Sixth week

Jog 880
Run 880, rest is 1:1
Run 2 440s, rest is 2:1
Run 2 220s, rest is 2:1
Run 2 100s, rest is 3:1
Run 7 60s, rest is 3:1
Run 7 40s, rest is 3:1
Run 7 20s, rest is 3:1

Summer Workout Schedule

Activity	Mon	Tue	Wed	Thu	Fri	Sat
Flexibility	x	x	x	x	x	x
Weight training	x		x		x	
Distance running: 2 to 3 miles	x		x			
Form running		x		x		x
Interval running*		x		x		x
Agilities and skill work by position		x		x		x
Recovery: light jogging; stretching hamstrings and shoulder girdle	x	x	x	x	x	x

*July and August

schools with similar numbers of players, philosophies, and resources. That's important because, as I said in chapter 3, our first goal every year is to be conference champion.

The key is to match your team with non-conference opponents against whom you can compete. Avoid schools that are too much bigger or too much smaller than yours. Sure, there's a chance you might play the role of David and slay some Goliath of a team, but at what price? Conversely, what good does it do your team to beat up on a noncompetitive, undermanned opponent?

 PAYING FOR SCHEDULING BIG

To gain exposure for our fine high school program, we once scheduled a school that had more students in one grade than we had in all four of our grades combined. The difference in size was apparent when we lined up on the field: They outweighed us by almost 30 pounds per man.

Still, we pulled out a victory, but at a great price. Our entire team was bruised and sore after facing players of such superior size and strength.

The following Friday we were fortunate to win, even though we played a much weaker opponent. We proved that we could play and defeat a much larger opponent, but it was apparent to me that we could not compete against that type of opponent every week.

If your team is not in a conference, scheduling can be difficult. Teams in conferences typically must commit at least two-thirds of their schedules to intraconference opponents. And when they do play outside their conference, they want to play at home.

Ideal Scheduling

I feel strongly about scheduling a big rival outside the conference. Everybody gets emotionally involved for such a game. Win or lose, we do not want to spend that emotion in a nonconference game, which has nothing to do with our primary goal of winning the conference.

The best schedule is to play half your games against opponents who match up fairly evenly against your team. The remaining half should be split among opponents who you feel are either slightly superior or slightly inferior to your squad. Try to avoid scheduling two inferior or two superior opponents consecutively. Ideally, your schedule might look like the one in Table 5.1. Realistically, with advance scheduling you never really know how good your opponents are going to be by the time that season rolls around.

Table 5.1   Sample Schedule

Game #	Site	Quality of opponent	Comments
1	Home	Weak	Nonconference
2	Away	Average	Nonconference
3	Home	Average	Conference
4	Away	Strong	Nonconference
5	Away	Weak	Conference
6	Home	Average	Conference, homecoming
7	Away	Average	Conference
8	Home	Strong	Conference, rival
9	Away	Weak	Conference
10	Home	Average	Conference

Try your best to project the quality of your opposition. Keep in mind that your players need good competition to grow. But be realistic. The emotional and physical cost of playing too many superior opponents can undermine players' motivation and development.

Discussing the Schedule With the Team

Players are perceptive and informed about how they are supposed to match up with their opponents, so don't try to fool them. Explain to them before the season that the coaching staff has one opponent only in mind each week, and that you expect them to take the same approach. Tell them to expect a straightforward assessment of their next opponent at the first team meeting of the practice week.

Unfortunately, many newspapers print point spreads and weekly "picks" of games. Your players will read these pregame predictions. If they take more stock in what a sportswriter says than what you say, you know you're in trouble.

Be honest when you describe the upcoming opponent's strengths and weaknesses. At the same time remind players that the opposing team is not the standard by which you measure their success. Instead, the yardstick is how their performance compares to their previous performances and performance potential.

Travel

A big consideration in planning a schedule is the amount of travel required. At the secondary school level, the distances you travel rarely require an overnight stay. Conference opponents are seldom more than a couple hours' bus ride away.

Bus Trips

No matter how short, bus rides can be miserable if you don't plan them. Here are some of the more important considerations to keep in mind when planning bus trips:

• *Bus and driver.* Whether you go by charter or school bus, make certain that the size and number of buses is sufficient. Also do whatever you can to ensure that the person behind the wheel is a dependable, responsible, pleasant, and reserved type.

• *Departure and arrival times.* Everyone on the traveling squad must be informed of when the bus leaves. Make it clear that you will permit no exceptions: Those absent when it's time to go will be left behind.

• *Seating.* Some coaches prefer to sit in the back of the bus so they can keep an eye on the players. Others choose to sit in the front. Seating has not been a problem for us. If we have more than one bus traveling to the game, I'd put the varsity on one bus and the freshmen and sophomores on the other.

• *Conduct.* If players understand how you expect them to behave, you shouldn't have discipline problems on the bus. If the team is focused, it should be fairly quiet on the way to any game. After a big victory, you might have to remind them to put celebrating on hold until you arrive home. Under all circumstances, players should leave the bus as clean as it was when they got aboard.

Overnight Stays

When college games and high school interconference and playoff games require traveling more than a few hours, it may be better to stay at a hotel near the stadium the night before the contest. You may be responsible for making the arrangements for rooms and meals. Make your plans early. Once the season begins, you don't want to spend much time confirming your plans.

Provide players with the hotel's address and phone number in case their families need to contact them. We assign players their roommates, usually by position so that they can talk about their responsibilities. Give them an itinerary for the trip, including "lights out" and meal times.

Staff Planning

Although players are the most important people in any football program, other personnel are crucial to the program's effectiveness. Here are the nonplayer positions that must be staffed before the season:

• Head coach and assistant coaches
• Medical professionals and student trainers
• Student managers
• Statisticians
• Videotape coordinator

Coaching Staff

Coaching staff sizes vary, depending on the size of the school and the level of play. When I began coaching at a small high school, I had only a three-man staff: I was the head coach, and we had a backfield coach and a line coach. All three of us worked with the offense, defense, and special teams. Several players were on all three units.

Now, at Augustana, we have a nine-man staff, and I don't think we could get by without each coach. Football has so many positions, on offense and defense, and each requires specific skills and different responsibilities. If you have several players at each position, as is the case at many high schools and colleges, you need enough coaches to provide adequate instruction.

Sample Coaching Staff

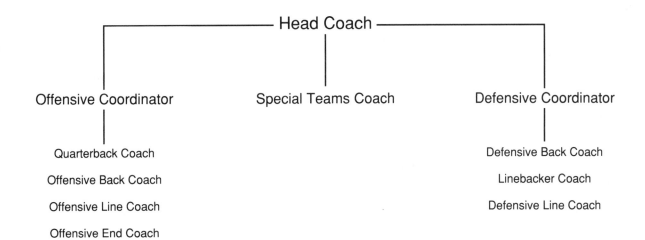

Preseason Coaching Staff Meeting

As I've said, it's vital that your staff work well together. So before the season, gather all the coaches and remind them of your philosophy and your expectations of their personal and professional behavior. Solicit questions and encourage questions to avoid or iron out problems.

Designating Staff Duties

The head coach must clearly define each staff member's duties. Once these duties are assigned, give the assistants the responsibility and let them coach. If a position coach knows he has a responsibility and the time allotted to teach the players at that position, he'll spend the time preparing.

To get the entire staff on the same page, tell every assistant what the other assistants are responsible for. That eliminates role confusion and gives everyone a greater appreciation of their colleagues' contributions.

Some duties may be covered by all coaches at various times during the season. For example, scouting assignments may rotate. Or, if you don't have a strength and conditioning coach available in the weight room, a different coach each week may be responsible for monitoring weightlifting.

Setting Up the Season Plan

Your preseason coaches' meeting should cover A to Z. Among the things you'll determine are

- practice times and formats,
- offense,
- defense, and
- special teams.

These four areas will be covered in chapter 6, under planning practices. Discuss each of these areas in detail before the season to clarify the staff's direction and emphasis in preparing the team.

Medical Professionals and Student Trainers

Earlier in this chapter, I emphasized the importance of having a team physician and athletic trainer. They may not help you with the Xs and Os, but you should treat them like part of the team—which they are. The medical staff can provide an invaluable contribution to the prevention, assessment, treatment, and rehabilitation of player injuries. Rely on their expertise and seek their input regularly.

Meet with the medical staff and student trainers, as a group or individually, before the season. Confirm schedules and responsibilities with them. Ask the athletic trainer to coordinate the student trainers' work and to maintain sufficient medical supplies.

Student Managers

Every football coach knows how smoothly a good group of student managers can make things go. Conversely, we know how badly things can go when student managers do a poor job.

Student managers are responsible for equipment and uniforms for home and away games. In college we have one man specifically assigned to care for all team equipment.

 FULLY EQUIPPED FOR SUCCESS

One year in high school, we had a freshman who wanted to be part of the program. He loved football but did not play. To our benefit, he became our equipment manager. He really enjoyed it and became so good that he chose it for a career. Today, Shorty Kleinan is head equipment manager at Kansas State University.

Here are qualities to look for in any student manager: high energy, dependability, honesty, and a positive attitude. A thick skin also helps, because managers often get grief from players. Never allow those barbs to be degrading or personal in nature. Players and coaches should treat all managers with respect.

Statisticians

Although we emphasize performance over numbers, statistics can help you spot weaknesses and strengths that your subjective observations miss. Our sports information department keeps our stats.

We keep all of the standard statistics, but here are the numbers that I probably put the most stock in (besides the point totals):

- Offensive production on first and second down, and third down conversions
- Special teams' yardage—gained versus allowed
- Defensive yardage allowed on first and second downs, and third down conversions at various distances

Videotape Coordinator

Football coaches, more so than coaches in any other sport, need to be able to review performances on tape. Those of you who, like me, were around before videotape and computers were introduced into football probably have old game films stored away that are so fuzzy you can hardly tell which team is which. Today's technology makes your analysis much easier.

However, you can't simply give any booster the equipment and be sure the job will get done. The key is to find someone who has the knowledge and skill to apply the technology and obtain the necessary footage.

Be sure to tell your video person which parts of the game are of greatest interest to you. Do you want all 22 players in the shot before the play begins? Should he focus the camera on defensive looks? What about close-ups of line play? Many programs now use two cameras to get footage of specific parts of the game.

Player Recruitment

I've had a chance to see colleges recruit high school football players from two perspectives: as a high school coach whose players were recruited by college coaches and as a college coach who recruits high school players to college. Being on one side (high school) for so long helped me determine how I would handle the other side.

The important thing is to plan ahead. Know the NCAA's rules about recruiting, the admission requirements, the periods when a player can and cannot be contacted by colleges, and so on.

As a High School Coach

One or more of your players may have the size and ability to play college ball. Choosing the school to attend is a tremendous decision for a young man. Everyone starts glad-handing him, saying how nice things will be—on and off the field—if he comes to their school. It's tough for a 17- or 18-year-old to keep things in perspective and make a rational decision. The boy often is just flattered to get the attention.

I tried to stay out of recruiting unless the player asked me to help. I did not want to interfere; it's the boy's decision, with input from his parents. When one of my high school players asked me to help him with the recruiting process, here's what I did and would recommend that other high school coaches do:

- Avoid steering him to any one school. Perhaps offer an opinion on the level of ball at which you believe he would be most challenged and successful. The size of the school never really matters if a young man gets to play and enjoys it.
- Tell him not to narrow the choice to one or two schools right away.
- Advise him to pick three or four schools that he has the strongest interest in attending, both for academics and athletics.
- Ask that he not play games with schools he has little interest in. If he takes the maximum number of visits just to take a plane trip or get treated like royalty by the schools, that will reflect poorly upon him and our program and hurt future players' chances of being recruited.
- Support the decision he makes if he follows these steps and involves his parents in the decision-making process.

Honesty the Best Policy

I was always completely honest with recruiters. If a recruiter asked what kind of prospects I had, and I felt we didn't have a Division I prospect, I would say so. This honest approach was beneficial because the recruiters learned they could trust my assessment. I didn't try to boost a player unless I felt the player could contribute to their program. The result was that our players always seemed to get scholarships when they deserved them.

Bucking the Odds

The chances of a high school football player's making the college or pro level are slim. The breakdown:

Number of high school players	927,000
Number of high school seniors	265,000
Number of NCAA players	47,000
Number of NCAA freshman positions	16,400
Number of pro rookies a year	215
Percentage of high school players who play in college	6.2
Percentage of college players who turn professional	2.4
Percentage of high school players who turn professional	<1.0

An important consideration is whether the college plays a style that would accentuate the player's skills. For example, if you have a great receiver who is small but catches everything thrown in his area, he might be happier in a system that calls for spreading the defense and passing a lot.

At the high school level, I tried to use a system diverse enough to get the most from our players' skills. If we had a good passing quarterback, he was going to get enough attempts—not to showcase him to colleges, but because it was best for the team.

As a College Coach

When I recruit, I first call the player's coach and ask to visit. I try to work around the player's schedule to find the most convenient time for the boy to talk with me.

I'm probably a poor recruiter because I hate to bother a kid, such as calling him every night. Sure, I could ask him how his school day was every day, but that shows disrespect for him and his free time.

  NO CLASS RECRUITING

My first experience with recruiting when I was a high school coach kind of soured me on the whole process. A recruiter from a big university called and insisted that I schedule a player to meet him at a time that was convenient for the recruiter but not for the player. Every morning, there would be a recruiter in the school hallway, talking to the player until the bell rang. So it ended up that the boy had almost no association with his peers. His senior year, which should have been the best time in his life, was suddenly over.

From then on I made recruiters work around the boys' schedules, not vice versa. And I vowed that when I became a college coach I would not disrupt recruits' schedules. If you pull a boy out of class often, it hurts his academic progress and his relations with classmates.

I call a kid only if I have something to tell him or ask him. For example, if a deadline for submitting financial aid requests is nearing and our school hasn't received anything from him, I might call to remind him and ask if he understands how the application process works.

Summary

You can never plan too much for a season. In this chapter we emphasized these key aspects of preseason planning:

1. *Equipment*—Football is a collision sport. Get your players the best helmet and shoulder pads possible.
2. *Conditioning*—The best prevention for injuries is good conditioning. Prepare your team for the physical demands of football before the first game.
3. *Scheduling*—Know your opponents. Make the regular season challenging but don't overschedule.
4. *Staff*—Get to know everyone on the staff and share responsibility with them. Keep in mind that the ultimate responsibility for the program is the head coach's.
5. *Recruiting*—Know the players in your program and those you are trying to recruit into your program. Help them reach positive decisions when they ask for help.

Chapter 6

Planning Practices

I've said before that practice is where you have to get down to business. And as in business, time is precious, attention to detail is essential, attitude is important, and organization is vital.

The business of practice is completed only through proper planning. You can't get it done just by jotting down some notes as your players take the field. Rather, your individual practice plans should be thoughtfully prepared and fit into your season master plan.

Practice Limits

Before describing our approach to practices, I'd like to say a few things about scheduling practices. The NCAA, in 1991, limited the amount of time Division I student-athletes

can devote to their sport to 20 hours per week. Many football coaches objected. And some coaches will probably continue to get more hours in, with excuses like "How can I help it if David takes our game tapes home and studies them 6 hours a day?"

High school coaches, too, have adopted this more-hours-are-better approach. They've set up mandatory year-round training programs, herding players into the weight room almost as soon as the gun sounds at their last game, and not letting up until they hit the practice field in August. "Skill position" players (receivers, backs, and quarterbacks) get time out for summer passing leagues to sharpen their skills and timing.

I disagree with scheduling practices throughout the year and taking up all of players' time during the season. Here are some reasons why.

First, if you do it, you're probably violating rules. Although no one agrees with all rules, we should abide by them. No one gains an advantage if everyone follows the same guidelines. So don't copy or worry about coaches who cheat.

Second, coaches who try to get ahead by practicing more hours than everybody else often discover it backfires. The players get sick and tired of hearing their coach yell at them for 12 months. After a while, the coach's voice doesn't have much impact.

Third, at the high school level, a young man should have the opportunity to compete in all sports. In high school and college, players should have a chance to develop socially and educationally away from football. For most, it won't be long before football is only a memory.

Many two-sport athletes have combined football and another sport. Deion Sanders and Bo Jackson are two recent athletes who played both pro baseball and football. But thousands of less famous college and high school athletes participate in multiple sports each year, with no apparent conflict. In fact, many times the skills required in one sport transfer well to the other.

HONDO AT QB?

Remember in the late '50s, when John Havlicek was deciding whether to play basketball or football in college? Woody Hayes tried to interest the All-State quarterback in joining the Ohio State football program, but "Hondo" chose the hardwood instead. The rest is history, as Havlicek went on to be an All-American with the Buckeyes and an All-Pro with the Celtics.

A fourth and very important point is that the premise of mandatory year-round practices is wrong, philosophically and psychologically. If part of the reason you're coaching is to develop kids' decision-making skills and to help them learn how to manage themselves and their time, then you're defeating that purpose. You're taking much of their time and making many of their decisions.

Finally, mandatory year-round programs don't let athletes or you know their real levels of motivation. We all know that athletes need to be self-motivated; they have to want to do it without someone always watching over them.

Practice Emphasis

We should limit the number of practice hours and days, but we can't do without practice. When it's time, it's time. And players must make a commitment to be there for each session and give maximum effort. By organizing well and not demanding all of the players' extra time, we feel we get maximum mental and physical effort from our team.

We show great respect for players who show up for every practice and work as hard as they can. By giving these players the most praise, other players learn the emphasis we place on practicing. And it's particularly important that the team's most talented players be leaders in practice. In fact, a big part of our success has been because talented players were eager to practice hard.

NO PRACTICE, NO LETTER

When I took my first coaching job, the high school had a rule about granting different colored letters to players based on their practice attendance. Players who attended every practice would receive a white letter. Players who missed one or more practices would receive a green letter.

My remark to that was, "If a player missed a practice, he will not play enough to letter." Obviously, there are some circumstances that prevent players from practicing. But I still subscribe to the belief that players earn their playing time—and letters—by practicing and practicing hard.

Preseason Practice Plan

The number of practices you are allowed to hold before the first game depends on the conference, state, or national rules governing your program. The NCAA allows 27 preseason practice opportunities. Before school begins, a practice opportunity is defined as two practices per day (excluding Sundays). After school is in session, a practice opportunity is defined as one per day.

High school rules vary regarding the number of practice days before the first game and the number of no-pads days to start out. In Illinois, you get 3 weeks of practice before the first game, with at least the first 3 days being without pads. For example, if the first game is set for September 3, then the first practice day is August 13, and players cannot suit up in pads before August 16. Anything you do to coach the team before the first practice date is illegal.

Our plan (in the appendix) for the preseason is to prepare the team completely—offense, defense, and special teams—so that we can have a formal intrasquad scrimmage one week before the first game. In a sense, we schedule Augustana first every year. This forces us to hurry some things, but we feel we can polish them later.

The first 3 days, we have the players practice without pads. Two-a-days are the norm for all programs during the first couple of weeks. I never felt our kids needed two practices on hot August days, but I was always afraid not to use the practice time available. If we were to lose the first game and had practiced once a day while the opponent practiced twice, I would have felt responsible—like I failed to do all I could to succeed. On the other hand, I think you need to be careful not to destroy players physically and mentally during this period.

As mentioned in the previous chapter, it is paramount that your players show up for preseason practices in good physical condition. Then, rather than having to devote extra practice time to conditioning, they can use the time to learn the system and hone their instincts and reactions under game-like conditions.

At the end of the preseason, your players should know your entire system. The offense, the defense, and special teams should be ready to go. And their focus should be on what they are going to do in the first game, not what the opponent will do.

Weekly Practice Plan

When preseason is over, we establish a weekly routine for preparing the team for the next game. Players like familiarity, and a regular schedule aids their learning.

The coaching staff has a standard weekly approach. First, we go over our preseason evaluation of the opponent. Then, if we have one, we look over the scouting report (chapter 15) to see if the opponent is doing things differently than we expected from our off-season evaluation.

Unlike our preseason practice planning, our weekly in-season planning emphasizes the opponent. Here's the day-by-day approach we took at the high school level.

Monday

We used this day to view with the team video of our previous week's game. We also gave to the players the scouting report on the opponent. Then we had the players get dressed in full gear and report to the game field. (Our junior varsity typically had Monday night games, so we usually had only our top two teams at the practice.)

We played the varsity against the sophomores in a passing scrimmage. This may seem strange for a team that thinks run first, but it let us improve our passing game against live, but not stiff, competition. It also gave us a chance to teach our line pass protection. And it gave our sophomores the best practice they could get against the pass.

    MORE BARK THAN BITE

As you might imagine, our seniors and juniors had some pride at stake in these Monday scrimmages. They didn't want a sophomore going around school the next day telling everyone how he had beaten the varsity on a particular play. So it was funny to see the reaction of a varsity lineman, for example, to getting beaten for a sack by a sophomore defensive lineman. No one had to point it out. All you had to do was look at the growling, steaming offensive lineman to know that it wasn't likely to happen again.

This was a full-contact scrimmage, but to avoid injuries to key varsity players and to keep our sophomores—who were very important to the program—from getting beaten up by bigger, stronger upperclassmen, we controlled it carefully. Players on both sides looked forward to these workouts.

Tuesday

This was a real work day, both for coaches and players. We would teach the parts of the offense and defense we planned to use against our next opponent and execute our

game plan against what we expected our opponents to use. Because the game was still 3 days away, we felt we could hit at full speed during part of this practice.

Tuesday practices were the week's longest, most intense, and most important. We believed that if we practiced poorly that day, we were in trouble for game day.

Although you might expect otherwise, our players actually liked Tuesday practices and approached them almost like games.

Wednesday

This was review day when the coaching staff and the players reexamined the game plan. The staff would ask: Is what we're doing clear to the players? Have we exposed and explained the opponent's strengths and weaknesses? Do we need to make further adjustments? Hopefully, at this point, we would be fine-tuning.

We might scrimmage parts of the game on Wednesdays. But if we did, we usually would use dummies on defense to prevent bruises. About the only thing we might do "live" would be to pass the ball against different defenses.

Thursday

This was dress rehearsal, lasting about 45 minutes. We had the team get into full gear and game uniforms. After stretching, we reviewed all personnel and replacements on special teams. We also reviewed and walked through defensive assignments. We ended

by having our offense run plays against no opposition.

I know some coaches choose not to have their players wear pads on the eve of a game, but we like the idea of keeping our players in a routine with some exercise and a shower. Plus, by having them dress in game uniforms, we're assured that each player will have his equipment ready to go the next day.

Weekly Practice Plan Summary

Monday
1. Review last week.
2. Make comments and corrections from game tape.
3. Run the weekend out of players' systems through the full-field passing scrimmage.

Tuesday
1. Work day.
2. Insert game plan.
3. Practice game plan live.
4. Check to see whether approach will work.

Wednesday
1. Review plan.
2. Make adjustments where necessary.
3. Work at full speed against players holding hand dummies.

Thursday
1. Dress rehearsal.
2. Work the special teams.
3. Review all assignments.

Friday
1. Play football!

Daily Practice Structure

We could set a tight daily practice structure in high school because we knew when everybody finished classes for the day, and we knew he had no place to go except to practice. So we could say, "Be on the field and ready to go 20 minutes after the end of last period." And when we blew the whistle to start, we could be confident that every player would be there. This regular starting time also allowed us to set a standard ending time.

Because college players have different class schedules, it's unrealistic to expect everyone to be on the field and ready to go when I blow the whistle. You have to work with whomever can make it at the regular time.

Whether you do or don't have a full squad, your daily practice plan must maximize the session for players who are present. That means working within the regular weekly practice routine and including important, standard components in each practice.

 DO NOT DISTURB

I have always found it necessary to leave my office and my telephone to concentrate on the practice plan each day. In the quiet for a few hours, I'm much better able to think through exactly what and how we should teach and practice that day. This focusing time lets me develop practices that run smoothly for the players and for our coaching staff.

The structure of our practices is always the same. Every practice session should include these components:

- Warm-up
- Conditioning
- Individual work
- Special teams play
- Offensive and defensive team play

If your players play both offense and defense, you'll need to separate the combined component.

Warm-Up Component

We use the warm-up period to prepare players for conditioning stations that follow. We jog a lap around the goals, then do stretching exercises.

Flexibility, the ability to move a muscle through a range of motion, is particularly important in injury prevention. As players perform these exercises, they should slowly stretch the muscle as far as they can without bouncing and should hold that position for 5 seconds. Players should do each exercise three times, stretching the muscle a little more with each repetition.

1. Stand with the legs crossed, and try to touch the forehead to the front knee. Recross the legs, putting the other leg in front, and repeat the stretch.

2. Stand with the legs spread apart, and try to touch the forehead to alternate knees.
3. Stand and place one foot on a base of support so that the leg is parallel to the ground. Touch the forehead to the knee, then repeat the stretch using the other leg.
4. Sit in a cross-legged position with the soles of the feet touching, and gently stretch the groin.
5. From a kneeling position, lean back and attempt to touch the head to the ground.
6. Sit in the hurdle position on the ground, touch the forehead to the knee, and then lay back.
7. From a standing position, lift the right heel toward the buttocks; grab the arch of that foot to deepen the stretch.
8. Rotate arms and shoulders in both directions.
9. Stand with the arms extended at the sides and the thumbs up. A partner stands behind the stretcher and slowly pulls the stretcher's hands back. Hold this stretch for 5 seconds, then bring the arms back to the starting position against an even resistance. Keep the arms at shoulder height throughout the entire movement.

10. Repeat the previous exercise with the thumbs down.
11. Kneel and place the hands behind the head. A partner stands behind the stretcher and braces his lower leg against the stretcher's back. The partner slowly pulls the stretcher's elbows back. Hold the position for 5 seconds, then bring the elbows back to the starting position against an even resistance.

Because all players are together in this period, it is a good opportunity to set the tone for practice and share important information the whole team should know. It's also a good time for the players to generate team spirit in preparation for the upcoming game.

Conditioning Component

We prefer to condition our team at the start of practice. Other coaches don't. We began this approach back in 1965. To be honest, I don't know whether conditioning players at the beginning of practice is best physiologically for the team. But in the 26 years that we've done it this way, we've lost just 27 games. You can see why we choose not to change.

We begin with a number of conditioning drill stations. At the high school level, we used six stations. At Augustana, we use eight. These stations are intended to develop strength, speed, hitting ability, and agility. The stations also increase the discipline and teamwork necessary to play in our system.

Conditioning Drill Stations

Here are the conditioning drill stations that we have used over the years. Some we performed as a team (t), others were performed in groups (g). The groups are determined by equal numbers, not by position. We spend 5 minutes on each. Choose at least five or six stations and try them as part of your practices' conditioning component.

1. Calisthenics (t)
2. Isometrics (g)
3. Dips, Chins, and Jump Rope (g)
4. Blaster™ (g)
5. High Stepper (g)
6. Weights (g)
7. Boards (g)
8. Form Running (g)
9. Tackling (g)
10. Hitting and Agility (g)
11. 40-Second Sprint (t)
12. Kicking (t)

1. Calisthenics

General exercises plus a lap around the field, followed by stretching. We then split into groups.

2. Isometrics

Used in high school where we had an isometric rack (see figure below). The bars of the rack are stationary and are at different heights to accommodate players of different sizes. All isometric exercises are done to a 10-second count.

3-foot bars: isometric and isontonic exercises, including curls, shoulder shrugs, and pull-ups from a supine position (keeping the body straight).

6-foot bars: isometric press and leg extensions with the arms straight.

8-foot bar: for pull-ups; player would jump up to the bar and pull himself up until the bar touched the back of his neck.

Dummy: Two players on opposite sides put the dummy into the V of their necks, lift the dummy from the ground, and hold it there for the required count.

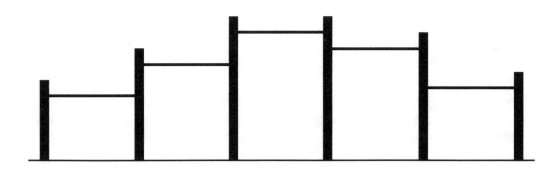

3. Dips, Chins, and Jump Rope

Dips: all the dips a player can do in 30 seconds

Chins: all the chins a player can do in 30 seconds

Jump Rope: jump 1 minute, rest 30 seconds, jump 1 minute.

4. Blaster™

Players run through to learn proper weight distribution and to improve their balance. Also good for backs and receivers to carry a football through it to emphasize strong grip and prevent fumbles.

5. High Stepper

All of the standard high stepper drills, such as hopping-speed and crossovers.

6. Weights

Weights built from concrete and pipe. Among the lifts: dead lifts, rows, shot snaps.

7. Boards

Boards 1 inch by 1 foot by 10 feet. Players first in line get in good stance and then can do any of a number of techniques:

- Sprint to end of board, hit the ground, roll, return to back of line. (Players should alternate direction of roll.)
- Put feet parallel to side of board. Pull the length of the board, face original direction, hit ground. (Repeat in other direction.)
- Two players are on one side of board and another faces them from the other side. Two players simulate offensive line blocking and drive other player to end of board.
- Player runs length of board to block player standing on opposite end (simulates blocking a linebacker).
- Two players on each side meet at board. Player to be tackled jumps and accepts blow delivered by tackler, who keeps eyes open and legs pumping while wrapping arms around player's midsection.

8. Form Running

Includes high step, bounding, etc. Coach keeps the group moving, whistling the start and end of each activity.

9. Tackling

Players line up 5 yards from one another, in a square. At the whistle, they tackle head-on or at an angle.

10. Hitting and Agility

Players perform any one of a number of agility drills, usually involving quick and high footwork over blocking pads. At the end of the agility moves the player makes a form hit on another player or a blocking pad.

11. 40-Second Sprints

Team lines up on one sideline and sprints to opposite sideline and back twice within 40 seconds. Everybody makes it.

12. Kicking

See chapter 14 on the kicking game.

We include a kicking game station to emphasize the importance of this part of the game to our players. While the team is learning and improving this part of our game, the players also get some great conditioning through repetitive sprints up and down the field.

Individual Component

During this component, each player works with his position coach. Most of our drills are conducted at this time. Drills are important because they allow players to get a lot of repetition in a controlled situation. This prevents most injuries.

The individual drill work focuses on techniques the player needs to perform effectively at his position. In the competitive part of the season, these drills often work on techniques especially important against the upcoming opponent.

Special Teams Component

We achieved our fine record only because we spent so much time on our kicking game. Don't neglect it; it's a third of the game.

We use this practice period to strengthen all special teams. We punt and cover every day, and as time permits we emphasize some other part of special teams relevant to the upcoming opponent.

Note that we also devote part of our conditioning period to the kicking game. This improves both our squad's physical training and its special teams execution.

Offensive and Defensive Team Component

When practicing as a team, we use our "scout" squads to simulate the opponent's offense and defense against our team. When you are not a two-platoon team, you must practice defense and offense separately for an equal time.

With a two-platoon team, you can practice offense at one end of the field and defense at the other. This is the time advantage of two-platoon football. It doubles the amount of time you can practice your offensive and defensive starters. You can't go completely two-platoon unless you have the players and the coaching staff to make it work.

Putting Practice Components Together

I've provided a sample practice plan (below) so you can see how we apply these practice

Sample Practice Plan		
Tuesday, October 5		
Offense	Defense	Other
Belly Perimeter with ends Goal line	Pass coverage Blitz Goal line	Warm-up Stations 40s Kickoffs

Time	Component	Activity or emphasis
3:30-3:45	Prepractice	Pass skeleton Belly options: 21 Sweep 37 Dive
3:45-3:55	Warm-up	Prepractice Stretching
3:55-4:10	Conditioning	Stations 40s
4:10-4:25	Special teams	Kickoffs
4:25-4:35	Walk through	Team walk and talk Outline the day 5-3 Autos
4:35-4:50	Individual work	Individual warm-up Position drills

4:50-5:50	Team offense and defense	Belly tight time and script
		Perimeter with ends
		Goal line: 23
		                 48 Reach
		                 36X
		                 23 Option Block

Comments:

1.

2.

3.

components. This plan is for a normal practice day.

I would encourage you to include all of the components in most of your practices. You can sequence practice components whatever way you feel is best for your team. Vary the order, the time allotted to each component, and activities within each component to emphasize a certain area or to add a little fun to the work routine.

Teaching During Practices

Identifying and sequencing practice components is vital to successful practices. But a plan is only as good as it is carried out. For me, the key to implementing a football practice plan is teaching.

We have time periods for each component, but we never hold our coaches to the exact time frame. Coaching is teaching, and if a coach needs some extra minutes to make his point, he has to have it. After all, if the players don't understand what to do, it won't get done. The coach has to take the time so they know what to do.

Our staff uses two primary teaching methods. We prefer the Praise First method, which goes something like this: "That's a good effort, but you could do . . . to make it even better." Players are more receptive to this method, because it challenges them and gives them information they can use to improve.

The second method is Scold and Reinstruct, such as, "Don't let your stance get so wide. The defender can knock you off balance easily in that position. Keep your feet shoulder-width apart." Players will sometimes respond poorly to the initial feedback. We don't like to leave a boy hung out to dry with a scolding. So we follow the negative comment immediately with the reason for making it and the correction.

Summary

1. The business of practice will get done only if you plan effectively.
2. Schedule practices legally and in the best interest of your players' overall development.
3. Develop a master plan that incorporates preseason, weekly, and daily practice objectives.
4. Make the most of practice time, and praise players who make the most of it.
5. Two-a-days are necessary evils during preseason, but guard against burning out your players.
6. The weekly routine should maximize the team's readiness for the upcoming opponent.
7. The daily plan should include standard components that cover all aspects of individual and team performance.
8. Even your best planned practices will benefit the players and team only if you teach effectively throughout them.

Part III

Coaching Offense

Chapter 7

Basic Offensive Positions and Formations

The Xs and Os. Chalk talks. Playbooks. Video analysis. People usually envision all those things when they think of coaching football.

Sometimes that stereotype is accurate: We do think a lot about how to maximize players' talent through correct positioning and effective play calling. But we also give a great deal of consideration to the concepts laid out in the first six chapters of this book. As a coach

you know that even the best football minds in coaching succeed only if they work effectively with players.

Assuming you have a handle on the concepts I've presented, you can focus on individual skills and team strategies that you'll teach your players. Let's begin on the offensive side of the line.

In this chapter, I'll briefly describe attributes to look for in players at each offensive position. Then we'll look at formations you might put these players in to start your team's offensive plays.

Player Positions and Skills

Since the days of the flying wedge and one-platoon squads, football has become a game of specialists. On each play, each player has a specific responsibility. To fulfill that responsibility, a player may require certain attributes and techniques. Therefore, in positioning your players, keep in mind the responsibilities, attributes, and skills typically associated with each offensive position (see Figure 7.1).

It is important to place your personnel in positions that maximize their talent in your offensive system and against the competition you're going to face. For example, because we're a Wing-T, run-first offense and most teams on our schedule play with an even defensive front, we may position our two strongest blocking linemen at the guards. Pro teams do the same thing, putting their best pass blocker at left tackle to protect the quarterback's blind side.

Center

The center's primary duty is to snap the ball to the quarterback to initiate each play. This exchange occurs in the form of a handoff of the football backward through the center's legs (see Figure 7.2). The center should turn the ball slightly as he snaps it to the quarterback, allowing the quarterback to grasp the ball with the fingers on the laces to hand off or pass quickly.

Figure 7.2 The center before snapping the ball to the quarterback.

In the shotgun or single-wing formations, the center must snap or pass the ball several yards through his legs back to the quarterback.

After delivering the ball to the quarterback, the center becomes a blocker. Because his blocking responsibilities usually involve a large noseguard or defensive tackle, a center needs to be big and strong. Quickness is an important attribute.

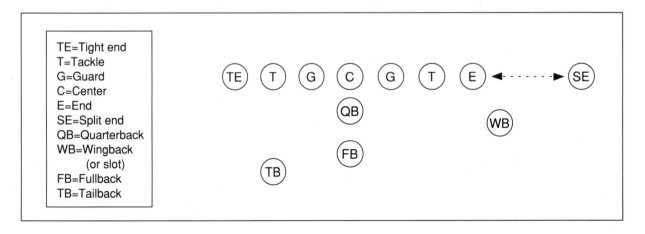

TE=Tight end
T=Tackle
G=Guard
C=Center
E=End
SE=Split end
QB=Quarterback
WB=Wingback
    (or slot)
FB=Fullback
TB=Tailback

Figure 7.1 Basic offensive positions.

The center also establishes the location of the huddle before each play. A lazy center can mean delay-of-game penalties, but a take-charge player at this position can mean increased offensive efficiency.

Guards

Positioned on each side of the center, the guards' overriding concern is to block defenders as designated for each play. Guards' blocking assignments vary greatly from one play to the next: Perhaps they'll trap on first down, pull on second, and pass block on third.

Because guards must make many types of blocks, they must be agile and well versed in a number of skills. These players also must be intelligent enough to remember their duties when plays are called. They also must think quickly when a breakdown occurs and an adjustment is necessary. Size is important to handle defensive tackles, as long as it doesn't compromise foot speed.

Tackles

Stationed outside the guards, tackles typically are the largest offensive linemen. Their size and strength help them perform their blocking assignments. Those assignments may be less diverse than those carried out by guards, but good blocking at the tackle position is vital to any successful line play.

As all linemen, tackles seem to be noticed most when they miss a block. All it takes is one bone-jarring, blind-side quarterback sack by a defensive end for an offensive tackle to get the attention of teammates, coaches, and fans.

But it's also important to recognize these linemen when they make their blocks. Big, strong tackles can drive holes into the defensive front and take on large defensive linemen who are trying to penetrate to the passer or ballcarrier. Good footwork is crucial for getting (and staying) in position to make the block.

Tight End

Think of a player who's not as big as a tackle, but who runs faster and catches passes like a split end. That player, the tight end, lines up on the line of scrimmage next to one of the tackles. On one play, the tight end may block like a tackle. But on the next play,

he may run a downfield pass route like a wide receiver.

It takes a good athlete to handle such a wide range of responsibilities. He must have sufficient size and strength to block opposing linebackers and linemen and also have the speed and hands to run routes and catch passes.

Split Ends

For the purposes of this book, I'll refer to all receivers who position themselves at the end of the offensive line, several yards from the tackle or tight end, as split ends. They also are commonly called wide-outs, wide receivers, or flankers.

Whatever the name, players in these positions should be among the quickest athletes on your team. They must be able to sprint down the field quickly and run effective pass routes or position block. The position block (or screenblock) requires the receiver to stay between the defensive back and the ball-carrier. And after the split end makes a reception, he must be able to run with the ball for yardage.

Running Backs

Running back is a general term referring to players who run the football after receiving a handoff or pitchout from the quarterback. The specific names, positions on the field, and responsibilities of running backs vary with offensive systems and sets.

The fullback generally lines up approximately 3 yards directly behind the quarterback. Strength is a great asset for fullbacks, who block for other runners and carry the ball on short-yardage plays. The fullback is a key to the success of many plays because he often sets up other runners with blocks or fakes.

The most common positions for a tailback are behind the fullback in the I-formation or to either side of the fullback in the deuce backfield. Some systems also place a halfback 1 yard outside and 1 yard behind the tight end or one of the tackles in a wingback position.

Because running the football is the halfback's chief duty, he must be fast and elusive. He also must be a workhorse, able to withstand hard tackles for four quarters and

to run just as hard at the end of the game as he did in the first series of downs.

Quarterback

If one football position calls out for a leader, it's quarterback. The QB calls the plays in the huddle, barks out the signals at the line of scrimmage, and takes the snap from center to start each play. From that point, the QB must be confident and have good ball-handling ability, including passing accuracy. The confidence will reflect his personality and his many hours of study that give him a total understanding of his offense and the opposing defense.

A quarterback need not be big, but he must be quick and have "escape ability." It is an advantage for the quarterback to be tall enough to see over linemen when looking downfield for open receivers.

Offensive Formations

There are as many offensive formations in football as the mind can conjure. It's like a math problem, where the teacher asks, "How many combinations of 11 people can you have if 7 must be on the line of scrimmage?"

Because the answers to that question are infinite, I've shown only the nine most common offensive formations in Figure 7.3, a-i. As you can see, from tackle to tackle the

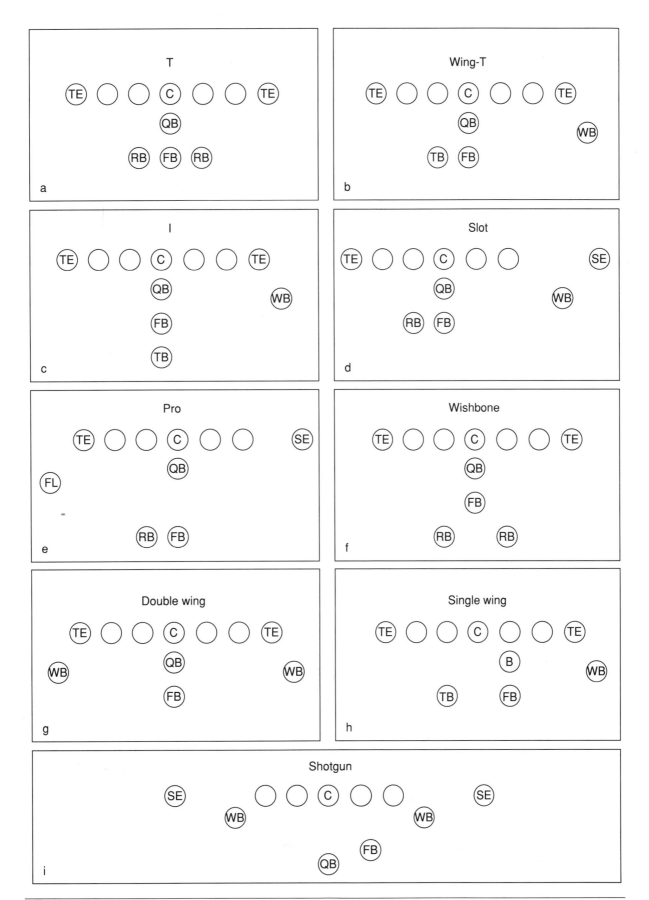

Figure 7.3 The nine most common offensive formations: (a) T, (b) Wing-T, (c) I, (d) slot, (e) pro, (f) wishbone, (g) double wing, (h) single wing, and (i) shotgun.

formations look similar (although the size of the splits between linemen will vary according to the system you use). But receivers and backs might set up in two very different formations from one play to the next. So the positioning of the receivers and backs is what distinguishes one set from another.

Choosing an Offensive Formation

Every coach likes some formations and dislikes others. For example, I have never liked the I-formation as a high school offense. It is too geared to having one back carry the ball 40 times. People now run a lot of variations out of the I-set, but in its original conception, the I-back was to get the ball 75% of the time. If you had an O.J. Simpson, an Archie Griffin, or a Herschel Walker, that was OK.

The problem is, not many high school coaches ever have such a talented runner. And even if you did have one excellent back around whom you centered the offense, what do you do when he gets injured?

A high school coach once told me the way to handle that problem is to rotate your best two backs as I-backs. Then each player can carry the ball every other down and not get tired. Just as important, if one player is injured, you still have an experienced, capable back on the field.

I thought it was such a good idea that I went to the three running back offense (one is actually a wing) that I still use today. That way it's hard for teams to key on any one runner, and it keeps my backs fresher, less susceptible to injury, and more involved in the team concept.

In a multiple-back attack, you can feature a great runner. The advantage is, you always have the option of going to the other two backs to keep the defense honest. Similarly, if you have a great quarterback, you can feature him and use the runners and receivers as secondary options.

The more I got to know about the wing formation, the better I liked it. And it has withstood the test of time. One of its primary values in a high school situation is that it allows you to feature the talent you have.

That also works in college. For example, in my first year at Augustana, we led the league in passing and receiving. That year

we had a good quarterback and a fine receiver, but because the system was new we could not properly execute the run.

Hybrid Formations

From the basic formations in Figure 7.3, coaches have developed sets that combine what they feel are the best two or three features. I doubt that the benefits of these hybrid formations (see Figure 7.4,a-d for samples) are as great as the coaches who use them think. But if they work, and the players on the team believe they will work, then the formations probably serve a purpose.

As you can see in Figures 7.3,a-i and 7.4,a-d, an offensive formation is simply that. We now describe an entire offensive system by only the formation, such as a wishbone offense or a pro offense. In fact, many coaches have written books based on this formation-equals-system approach.

    LONGHORN MATERIAL?

In 1962, my first year at Geneseo High School, we were running our entire offense from a T-formation. Our fullback was also our starting defensive tackle. That meant he had to go all out on every play.

Some 10 years later, while putting together a highlight film of our state record winning string, I reviewed a tape of one of our '62 team's games. I noticed, for the first time, that our fullback, as he tired late in the game, moved up closer to the quarterback as he got in his stance. So, in the second half of most of those games, we became a wishbone team.

Funny thing was that the term *wishbone* was not coined until the late '60s. If only I had been smart enough to write a book then and use the name wishbone for our offensive system, maybe Darrell Royal would have hired me!

Two Philosophies on Formations

Generally, coaches take two different approaches in adopting an offensive formation. One is to load up an area with a tight formation: two tight ends, three running backs, possibly an unbalanced line. The other approach is to spread the players out with multiple wide-outs, perhaps only one running back, and perhaps no tight end.

The tight formation is best for simple, power football. You're basically telling the

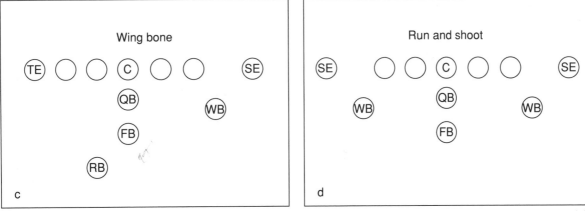

Figure 7.4   Four hybrid offensive formations: (a) Pro-I, (b) split-back twin, (c) wing bone, and (d) run and shoot (aka the double wing–double flex).

defense it is going to have to stop the run to stop your team from scoring. And that isn't always easy to do, because the tight formation allows you to set up two-on-one line-blocking schemes and to have lead blocking backs for ballcarriers.

On the other hand, a tight formation takes away from an offense's big-play potential. By it's very nature, it's a ball possession offensive attack. A tight formation also can let the defense stack players at the line of scrimmage and match its strength with your offense's strength.

The big-play potential is always present with a spread attack. By making the defense cover sideline to sideline, the spread formation allows great individual athletes at the skill positions to maneuver against isolated defenders in the open field. The Barry Sanders type, who is almost impossible for one defender to stop, makes this formation excel. (Actually, a back as good as Sanders would make any formation effective.)

If you don't have speed and talent at the skill positions, the spread formation may not be a good choice. You also must have a quarterback with good arm strength who can zip the ball to receivers running routes downfield and to the sidelines. And your linemen must be able to block one-on-one, because they aren't going to have any help on most plays.

Comment on Formations

A sound formation allows for a balanced offensive attack. From it, your team should be able to run and pass effectively. Moreover, the formation should allow your team to take advantage of its strengths and hide its weaknesses.

You will find that the great programs in sports history are those that have had balance and were consistent. Lombardi turned his pro football teams into error-free machines. UCLA basketball, under John

Wooden, had a consistent style of play, even though it went from perimeter-oriented teams to post-oriented teams and back again. The basic approach was always the same: They featured who they had.

In present-day Division I football, you see a similar type of consistency among programs with the same coaches in charge for several years. Nebraska, Penn State, and Florida State differ in their styles of play, but within their football programs they teach players one way to play the game, consistently. And that identification and belief in a system gives the players who attend those schools great confidence.

Some coaches go from a wishbone to an "I" and back and forth, but that isn't a basic change; that is only a formation change. They still didn't change their idea of what they wanted.

Summary

1. Coaches of consistently successful football programs find the best possible positions for each of their players, then teach them the individual position skills and team tactics to contribute to the overall effort.

2. To help you assign your players to their best roles, I described the general attributes to look for in designating players for each offensive position.

3. Once you know your personnel and their positions, you need to determine what offensive formations will optimize their performance.

4. The formations to choose from are limited only by imagination. Each is as good as the personnel you have executing the offense.

5. A team with good, big linemen but a shortage of speed and talent at the running back and receiver positions may be better off using a tight formation.

6. A team loaded with speed and athletic ability might be most successful from one of the spread formations.

7. Whatever offensive formation you choose, remember that the alignment of players on the field is important only if they have the tools to make it work. Chapter 8 will help you make sure they do.

Chapter 8

Teaching Offensive Skills

In most sports, coaches are recognized for their outstanding ability to teach their athletes performance techniques. Not so with football coaches. Instead, people attribute our success to tactical decisions, genius play calling, special teams preparation, or some other team-related aspect.

That's a shame because anyone who knows our sport and what it takes to be a successful coach realizes that individual instruction is the foundation for developing any effective team effort. The Xs and Os that even the most brilliant strategist devises aren't worth much if his players don't have the skills to take them from the chalkboard to the playing field.

In this chapter, I'll cover the basic techniques football players need to know to contribute to a team offense. I won't emphasize how to perform the skills as much as I will how to teach them effectively.

Some of you may consider this a simplistic presentation. To you I say: In teaching football skills, the simpler you keep it, the better. Here's a position-by-position look at how to teach offensive skills.

Offensive Linemen Skills

All of us have blocking schemes that look good on paper. The right tackle kicks out the

81

defensive end. The right guard screens the inside linebacker. The center blocks the noseguard. And just like that, your fullback waltzes into the end zone.

That's the way it's *supposed* to work. But this domino effect on the defense won't happen if your offensive linemen haven't been taught the proper fundamentals.

Stance

Start by emphasizing proper offensive line stance. Emphasize it every day, every play.

A good, comfortable stance is the basis for correct and effective line blocking. Interior linemen usually assume a three-point or a four-point stance. We prefer a four-point stance because most of our offensive plays are designed to have the linemen block forward.

A lineman's feet should be shoulder-width apart with toes pointing forward. The feet can be staggered slightly, but no more than a heel-to-toe relationship. Generally, the linemen will want to stagger their feet according to their dominant hand; right foot back for right-handed players; left foot back for lefties.

As the player squats, his hands drop to the ground, his head goes up and his eyes look forward (see Figure 8.1). The weight of the body should be balanced with the legs and feet so that the player will not need to take a "false" step to correct a weight imbalance before executing his assignment.

The center has a bit different stance because of his snapping responsibility. His feet

Figure 8.1 A four-point stance for an offensive lineman.

must not be staggered more than toe to instep. A long stagger could cause problems with alignment and make it more difficult for the quarterback to pull away after receiving the snap.

Balance and control of the football are the key fundamentals for the center. His ability to hand the ball to the quarterback in a quick, safe manner and to move in any direction after the snap makes this position vital to consistent offensive play.

Base Block

At some point, offensive linemen must earn their keep by blocking a defender one-on-one. Therefore, you must spend time with your linemen to master the base block.

With rules changes allowing more freedom in the use of hands, many coaches now teach their linemen to use professional techniques like blocking high with an open hand, similar to a bench press.

Here are basic blocking techniques I recommend teaching your players:

1. In a good stance, the player's eyes should focus on the numbers of the opponent's jersey.
2. On the snap count, have the player explode forward, lifting his hands from the ground with the eyes focused on the numbers and the shoulder aimed at the opponent's numbers while bringing his hands up from the ground. This action makes it possible for the blocker to drive his hips underneath and lift and run at the same time.
3. As when lifting a heavy load, the player should then take short steps and keep a wide base to maintain balance.

You can teach this sequence using a blocking dummy or, as we like to teach it, against another player in a "fit" position (see Figure 8.2). The defensive player takes the "fit" position by putting the right leg forward, putting the right arm in front of the right leg, and bending over (as if holding a hand shield). This gives the offensive lineman a perfect target for blocking.

Teaching the base block against another player rather than a blocking dummy is much better because it simulates live contact. Hitting only dummies may prepare players well for a pillow fight, but it doesn't

Figure 8.2 An offensive lineman in a base block against a defender.

give them the feel for crashing into a defender. This is especially helpful to really young players.

As you can tell, we do not emphasize the professional blocking technique with the hands. We believe the only time a lineman should extend his arms within the frame of the body is when he is maintaining (not establishing) control of the opponent as the defender tries to separate and pursue.

Teaching the open hand "bench press" block to a high school lineman typically results in the player getting too high in the stance too early during the block. When this happens, the defender can easily overpower the lineman by driving right through his hands.

Pull and Trap Block

Your system may not call for your offensive linemen to pull much. Nevertheless, I encourage you to teach pulling and trap blocking for conditioning, agility development, and run blocking purposes.

The key when teaching linemen to pull and trap is to move quickly across the formation and to remain low to the ground so that they can block an opponent at any time.

We teach the "pull step," where the lineman turns the foot on the side he intends to go, swings the arm on that side of the body back, pivots the opposite foot in the same direction, and runs. As the lineman makes his turn, he also should turn his head to look in the direction he plans to run.

Younger players seem to learn this technique more quickly if you emphasize the head turn and arm swing instead of the footwork involved. That will get them into a position to attack without them having to worry about the step and pivot.

Cross Block

Most blocks that offensive linemen perform are made within an offensive blocking scheme. An example of this is the cross block, which involves two linemen taking on two defensive players.

To teach the cross block, line up the blockers side by side. Have the outside lineman make the first move, which will be toward the defender stationed across from his teammate. The inside lineman will pull behind this block and take on the defender to the outside (see Figure 8.3).

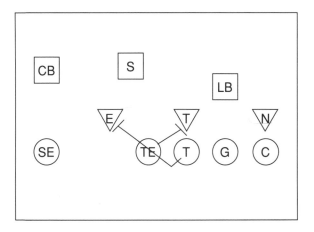

Figure 8.3 The tackle and tight end execute a cross block.

The key is to teach the outside offensive lineman to blow out of his stance quickly and to cut off the inside defensive lineman. We teach this lead blocker to aim for his blocking mate's helmet. That is the approximate area the defender will be in when he charges forward. And by the time the outside offensive lineman reaches that point, the inside offensive lineman will have pulled his head back and turned to make the block on the outside defender.

Fold Block

The fold block is similar to the cross block, except the roles of the two linemen are reversed. The inside offensive lineman makes the first move, blocking the outside defender. The outside offensive lineman then will "fold" or "pull" toward the inside. In our thinking the "fold" is only a term used to cross block with the inside man first, then the outside man. A pull or trap block begins with the outside man and follows with the inside.

Pass Block

We've focused on run blocking techniques to this point. In fact, many of these techniques also can be used by linemen on play-action pass plays.

However, to pass protect effectively in a drop-back passing scheme, an offensive lineman must employ a different technique. Here is the basic pass blocking sequence to teach players:

1. Step back off the line on the snap.
2. Stay low, with knees bent and head up.
3. Deliver a stronghand shiver to the opponent's number.
4. Separate from the defender, shuffling your feet and keeping your back numbers aimed at your quarterback.

5. Resume the low stance and repeat the sequence.

Emphasize the importance of offensive linemen staying aware of the quarterback's position. Obviously, the lineman's job is to remain between the defender and the quarterback. To do so, he must be alert and keep his feet moving.

Offensive Line Drills

Fit Drill

Purpose. To teach the fundamental progression of the straight-ahead base block

Procedure. Line up two, three, or four defenders in a standing fit position (explained in base block). Then have two, three, or four offensive linemen face them, in a good stance with normal splits between each other. On the snap count the offensive players perform a basic drive block, exploding to the left or right and following through with their legs.

Coaching Points. Check for the proper stance, for the false step, and for the use of legs in the follow-through. This is also a good drill to teach linemen to get off the ball quickly. This drill is very similar to group sled blocking, but young, inexperienced

players benefit more from blocking a real player.

2-on-2 Drill/3-on-3 Drill

Purpose. To practice all the types of blocking you plan to teach in a group small enough that you can see everything taking place and make all necessary corrections

Procedure. Two defenders face against two offensive linemen (or 3-on-3). The coach stands behind the defense where he will signal to the offense what type of block they will practice—straight-ahead drive block, cross block (first man signaled goes first), pass block, or trap block, especially with 3-on-3. On the command the defense will charge straight ahead and react to the offensive block.

Coaching Points. This is a full-speed line block that enables the coach to watch each player and to find players who can control another player under the most difficult conditions.

Tight End Skills

The tight end, as described in chapter 7, is the most "athletic tackle" in your program. Because of his dual role as a blocker and pass receiver, he will drill with both the linemen and the split ends.

First, your tight ends must have the strength and ability to block defensive tackles. The blocking techniques are the same as those described for other offensive linemen.

Second, tight ends must learn to release from the line of scrimmage on pass plays. One technique is the power move, where the tight end explodes through the defender and tries to inhibit his release. The other technique is a finesse move, involving a jab step as in basketball and a swim technique as taught to a defensive lineman.

Split End Skills

Split ends also have blocking responsibilities. In particular, most wide-outs are asked to position block downfield should a ballcarrier break free. The quality of such downfield blocks can mean the difference between a touchdown and a first down.

The position block is really nothing more than shielding a defender from the ballcarrier. The key is to drive hard off the line of scrimmage to force the defense to backpedal. When the defensive back stops, the receiver breaks down (runs under control) and "mirrors" the defensive back. As you watch your receivers attempt this block, make certain they don't hold or clip, which is even worse than not trying to block at all.

Most of your individual instruction with receivers will focus on how to run pass patterns and catch the football. That's what they like to do, and that's how they earn their keep.

Getting Off the Line

The first skill to teach your split ends is to get off the line of scrimmage and into their pass routes as fast as possible. When you teach this burst-and-escape move, encourage your split ends to read and anticipate what the defender will try to do to hold them up at the line. Receivers should master moves to counter whatever technique the defender uses.

Most offensive systems have their wide receivers take a two-point stance, knees slightly bent and feet staggered. This position allows the receiver to move quickly and to be ready to catch the ball as soon as the quarterback gets it from the center.

Running Routes

The first three steps a split end takes should put him into his pass pattern. As you work with receivers, emphasize that running a good pass route requires more than just moving to a specific spot on the field. Yes, receivers have to reach designated areas on each play, but even more importantly they must elude defensive coverage so the quarterback can deliver the ball to them.

For eluding defensive backs, teach your receivers head-and-shoulder fakes, change-of-pace, and other deceptive moves. Also use pass routes that will put distance between them and the coverage. In addition, work with your receivers on the mental side of the game. Explain that in their cat-and-mouse game with defensive backs, their moves can't be too predictable or the defenders will have the advantage.

Catching the Ball

Although escaping quickly from the line and getting open are very important, great receivers are great receivers because they *catch* the ball when it is thrown in their vicinity. The one thing that all great receivers I've coached have had in common is the ability to concentrate solely on the ball until they have it in their hands.

 IMMACULATE RECEIVER

One receiver especially good at focusing totally on the ball was Barry Pearson. Barry was an All-State running back in high school and became an All-Big Ten receiver at Northwestern. He played 5 years of professional football with the Pittsburgh Steelers and the Kansas City Chiefs.

Barry was just 5-11 and 185 lb, and his 40-yard dash time was only 4.6 seconds. In other words, he wasn't the prototype, speedy pro flanker. But, as Steelers receivers coach Lionel Taylor said, Barry was smart, could get open, and would catch the ball.

Despite having such a great career, Barry will probably be best remembered by sports trivia experts as the intended receiver in the famous "immaculate reception" play that Franco Harris made for the Steelers in 1975 to beat the Raiders.

A receiver should use the hands—not the arms, and not the body—to catch the ball. Although it may seem far-fetched, an effective way to teach receivers to use their hands is to have them practice catching a Nerf football. If they try to use their body or arms, the foam ball will bounce off. After a while, receivers will learn that hands-only catches are the most successful.

One thing you can't teach receivers is a "sense" or "nose" for the football. Even if they run great routes and get some distance from their defender, it won't do any good unless they want the ball more than the defense does when it's thrown their way. Related to that is an ability to catch the ball in traffic. Any veteran receiver knows that 9 times out of 10 you're going to get hit when you try to make a catch. Receivers who can't "go over

the middle" really limit what your team can do offensively. On the other hand, a receiver who has no apprehension about sticking his nose into the heart of the defense is a great weapon.

 A SPECIAL SKILL

Norm Singbush, MVP on our 1978 state championship team, MVP in the 1983 national championship game, and a 1984 Division III All-American, was one of the toughest wide receivers I've had the pleasure to coach. Norm was 6-1, 180 pounds, and ran a 4.75 forty-yard dash. In other words, he wasn't very big or very fast.

But Norm, very simply, was a great receiver. No matter what kind of coverages he faced, he always got open. And when the ball was thrown in his direction, he did not drop it.

It was as if Norm had feelers on when he went for a catch. This special skill came from practice, courage, and the ability to relax and accept the contact at the time of the catch.

To be great, receivers must practice a lot and concentrate when they practice. Anyone can catch a football in the backyard when no one is around. Real receivers can catch a football and relax and hold onto it regardless of what contact follows. There's one thing that receivers, like backs, can be sure of: When they have the ball, they'll draw a crowd.

Receiver Drills

Catch-and-Tuck Drill

Purpose. To teach the proper catching of the ball in the hands and to tuck the ball into the body so not to fumble

Procedure. Throw the ball to your receiver at different levels and teach him to reach for the ball with the thumbs in, catch the ball, and pull it to the body.

Coaching Points. As players master the catch and tuck parts of the drill, have them work on running a crisp pass route and then making their first quick move and sprint after tucking the ball in—a great warm-up drill!

Release, Go, Jump, Catch

Purpose. To teach the receiver to release from the line and to catch with a defender at the highest point

Procedure. Receiver lines up against a defender, who is in bump-and-run position. Receiver beats the defender off the line with a fake or swim move, then runs a route upfield. The quarterback throws the ball high so the receiver can outjump the defender.

Coaching Points. This is a good drill for the receiver and the defender. Both must concentrate on the flight of the ball while still respecting each other's vertical plane. The receiver should try to catch the ball at its highest point and hold on.

Running Back Skills

You'll teach fullbacks and halfbacks many of the same skills. Because their roles differ, you'll also teach them position-specific techniques.

Stance

For example, depending on the formation you use, the fullback may begin in a four-point (e.g., wishbone) or three-point stance; the halfback always will start from a three-point or two-point (e.g., "I" or Delaware Wing-T) stance. The key is whether your system requires a lot of lateral movement in the backfield. If so, the fullback will likely be in a three-point stance and the halfback in a two-point stance.

Generally speaking, you'll teach running backs to keep their feet closer together than you did with linemen. Much like a sprinter in track, you want your backs to be nearly full speed on the first step. However, you'll not want your running backs to put as much weight on their hands as a sprinter in the starting blocks. The reason? A back must be immediately ready to handle the ball and read the defense; the sprinter has to be concerned only about staying in a lane.

Taking Handoffs

Some coaches teach running backs to take handoffs with the hands open like a baseball player catching a ball below the waist. This allows the back to take the ball and hand it off again or to cradle it for running.

We prefer to teach our backs to put the elbow closest to the quarterback flexed up near the chest and the *palm of that hand turned forward.* The opposite elbow should be flexed near the belt with the palm up. When the the quarterback places the ball between the running back's arms, the back cradles the ball in both arms. In the first method, the back will *get the ball and run.* In the second, the back *runs and gets the ball.*

The cradle method of taking handoffs reduces the number of fumbles, both during and after the exchange. It is particularly helpful near the line of scrimmage where contact could be made immediately, because the running back covers up the ball by cupping his top arm and hand over the top of it.

Finding the Hole

Once the back has the handoff, his next priority, as Lombardi and many other coaches have said, is to "run to daylight." If your blocking scheme has worked, that daylight should be in a designated hole in the line. Teach your backs to look for this hole and hit it as quickly as possible.

To avoid fumbling, the ballcarrier must at all times protect the ball. He should always carry the ball in the hand away from the nearest defender, cover the tip of the ball

with both hands on contact, knowing that the defense will try to take the ball away if possible.

When running in open field, the back can allow the ball to come away from the body slightly so that he can use his arms to run. However, the back must squeeze the ball into his body when in traffic.

Running Back Drills

Handoff Drill

Purpose.   To teach backs to form a proper pocket with the inside arm up, then squeeze the ball when it's handed off

Procedure.   Two lines face each other. The ball is in one line and is handed to the other line as the two lines move toward each other. As one back receives the ball, he hands it back to the next runner. Players change lines to practice taking handoffs from both sides.

Coaching Points.   Watch players' arm positions, making sure the inside arm is up and the elbow is out of the way. As players get more sure-handed have them pick up the pace until they are running as fast as they will in live action.

Fumble Drill

Purpose.   To teach running backs to protect the ball and not to fumble on contact

Procedure.   Line up two lines in a "tunnel" arrangement. Have ballcarriers run through the tunnel at full speed, with a football in each arm. Players on both sides of the tunnel try to strip the footballs from the runners.

Coaching Points.   Having to protect two footballs simultaneously forces the runner to concentrate and to squeeze the balls into his body.

Quarterback Skills

The quarterback stance you'll teach will vary according to your style of offense. First and foremost, teach your quarterback to get into a position that allows for the smoothest exchange from the center.

Taking Snaps

What may seem like a minor point isn't so minor when the quarterback fails to get a snap from center and it costs your team a possession—or even a game. The center-quarterback exchange must be automatic. To make it automatic takes repetition of proper mechanics. Here's how we teach our quarterbacks to receive the snap:

1. Put your hands under the center's buttocks with the throwing hand as the top hand.
2. Bend the arms slightly to allow for extension as the center initiates the snap. Also press the top hand against the center so that the center can feel the

hand's position and so the quarterback can follow the center as he moves.

3. The quarterback will receive the ball with the laces in the throwing hand, in position to throw.

 A HANDS-DOWN WINNER

We had always taught our quarterbacks to put the throwing hand as the top hand under center until 1983. That year our quarterback, Jay Penney, indicated that he had always placed his nonthrowing hand on top. He felt that the ball would strike his off hand hard from the center and that he could more quickly control the ball with his strong hand.

Our coaching staff decided that we should let Jay continue to use the technique that had worked for him through his high school and early college career. Better not to mess with a good thing, even if it's a little unorthodox. And Jay's performance was better than good. He quarterbacked our team to the national championship that year.

The quarterback must be able to control the ball and move quickly. First, he pulls the ball close to his body like a poker player and then hands off or passes as deftly as an experienced dealer.

Handoffs

The handoff is the quarterback's responsibility. If the running back uses good technique (see previous section) to receive the handoff, it's up to the quarterback to deliver the ball into the ballcarrier's belly.

Timing and spacing are very important. Proper timing is a matter of practice. Spacing has more to do with formation. Too close and the backs will collide. Too far from each other and the quarterback won't be able to get it to the intended runner.

Assuming that timing and spacing are good, the quarterback should place the ball under the running back's inside elbow and hold onto it until he feels the back grasp it.

Pitchouts

Plays designed to get a running back the ball quickly, or to get it to the back at a position that prevents the quarterback from handing off, often use a pitchout. The pitchout is an integral part of an option offense.

The most commonly used option pitch is similar to the one-handed chest pass in basketball. It allows for a soft pass that can be handled easily, yet one that gets to the back quickly. The key for any option quarterback is to make sure that he leads the trailing back so that the ballcarrier does not have to break stride waiting for the ball.

The shovel pitch is often used when the quarterback pitches to the back from a stationary position. One example of this is the quick pitch, a play that was more popular during the '60s.

Passes

If your team throws the ball a lot, you know how important it is to teach quarterbacks correct passing techniques. Even if you emphasize the running game, your quarterbacks must be able to pass the football to prevent defenses from stacking the line of scrimmage.

Throwing the football differs from throwing the baseball in several ways. First, the quarterback doesn't have the luxury of standing high on a mound, pushing off a rubber, and taking his sweet time like a pitcher. Instead, he must run to the spot from which to throw, drop, sprint, roll, gather himself, get rid of the ball before the defense sacks him, and hope no one deflects or intercepts the ball on its flight to the intended receiver.

Second, the target (receiver) to whom he is throwing is rarely stationary as is a baseball catcher. The receiver may be downfield, coming back for the ball, or moving across the field in either direction. You must help your QBs develop a feel for the distance and speed required.

Third, the QB should release the ball near the ear, with a follow-through similar to a free-throw shooter. A round-house pitching type motion not only takes much longer and exposes the ball to rushing defenders, but produces less accurate and less consistent passes.

Fourth, there is no strike zone. In fact, the best pass in a given situation might be called a ball by a home plate umpire. A QB may have to throw the ball above the receiver's head for the pass to be completed over a nearby defender.

Quarterback Drills

Set Up And Release Drill

Purpose. To teach quarterbacks to set up quickly and prepare to throw the ball when the receiver breaks

Procedure. Line up quarterbacks facing each other, 10 to 15 yards apart. At the snap, the quarterback rolls out, sprints out, or drops back (3, 5, or 7 yards) as quickly as possible; sets up; and on the coach's whistle throws the ball to his quarterback partner. The partner follows the same procedure and delivers a return pass.

Coaching Points. This teaches quarterbacks first to set up quickly and then to release the ball in a split-second. Also, by correcting and instructing one quarterback in the presence of the others, you are teaching all your quarterbacks important techniques at the same time.

Option Pitch Drill

Purpose. To teach the technique of the option pitch

Procedure. Two quarterbacks 6 to 7 yards apart run side by side across the field. Have the one with the ball stop, set his feet, and pitch the ball to the other quarterback, who continues to run. Once he delivers the ball, the stopped quarterback hustles to catch up, at which point the second quarterback stops, sets his feet, and pitches the ball back to the first quarterback.

Coaching Points. The players' return trip across the field allows for use of the other hand.

<u>Summary</u>

1. No matter what the size, speed, or body build, a good lineman must learn to control a defender one-on-one.
2. Receivers must be able and willing to catch the ball. You can improve their ability by teaching them to grasp the ball with their hands.
3. Running backs are typically your most skilled athletes. Don't let that talent go to waste. Teach them to concentrate when they handle the ball.
4. The quarterback is the point guard of the offense. He must be a confident and capable leader.

Chapter 9

Teaching the Running Game

People call me a "run-first" coach. They're right. And here's a little story that sums up why I prefer the ground game.

Several years ago at the American Football Coaches Association's annual convention, the featured speaker pointed out that "of the top 15 running teams in the nation, 14 had winning records and all of their coaches were rehired." Nothing surprising there. But he then noted, "Of the top 15 passing teams, only 5 had winning records, and 7 coaches of those 15 teams lost their jobs."

That speech probably opened some coaches' eyes to the importance of running the football, if for no other reason than job security. I have my own reasons for choosing a run-first philosophy:

- The programs dominant in the history of football were founded on the run-first offense: Lombardi at Green Bay, Paterno at Penn State, and so on.
- A run-oriented offense is less prone to turnovers.
- The total running game, when you consider the blocking skills involved, is easier to teach in limited time. This factor is especially important in one-platoon high school football.

- Running the football keeps the clock moving and puts your team in control of the game. This style tends to wear down opponents.
- Probably the best reason we choose to run first is that we know the running game, and we can therefore teach it better.

Establishing a Running Game

To run the football successfully you must have a plan, a system. You have to believe in that system totally. And you have to know it inside and out.

You can teach a system to players only if you understand it and are committed to it. Then it's a matter of getting them to believe in the system and to be motivated about running the football.

The organization of this chapter follows the thinking a coach must do in developing an effective ground attack. Begin by identifying a base formation. Then decide what type of running plays your team is most capable of executing. And from that decision you'll implement a system, including specific plays and terminology for them.

Selecting a Run Formation

Very simply, the way you line up your offense is a formation. The formation includes all 11 players, with at least 7 on the line of scrimmage.

Keep in mind that formations are *not* offenses. We, as coaches, get in the habit of labeling our offenses by the way they line up. We talk about a wishbone offense or a pro offense, when really we are describing only the arrangement of players.

You can use a variety of formations to run the same offense. And as we all know, more formations are being used today than ever before.

The key is to choose formations that offer the most advantages to your personnel. Let's look at four classic offensive formations and their strengths and weaknesses.

Wishbone

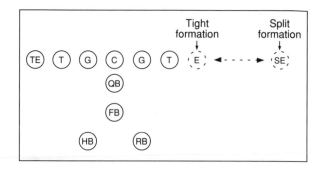

The wishbone has been used very effectively, perhaps never more so than by Darrell Royal's teams at the University of Texas in the early '70s. Emory Bellard is credited for first using this formation in Texas high schools.

No pro team uses the wishbone, and only a handful of Division I schools do. But the offense is favored by several middle-division schools and many high schools.

The wishbone can be a real asset to teams that have speed, but not necessarily size. Also, the option offense that is typically run from the wishbone is relatively safe—free of turnovers. The wishbone is especially effective if you have a great runner at quarterback.

The wishbone's drawback is that it does not allow for many misdirection plays. Opponents also tend to stack the line of scrimmage against this offense, recognizing the limited number of quick receivers available for passes.

I-Formation

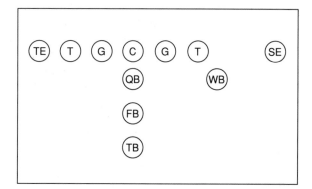

The I-formation was an outgrowth of the belief that if you could get your best running back deep behind a blocking fullback, the running back could run for daylight to any area on the field—right, left, or middle. That's why Auburn University switched from the wishbone to the "I" when Bo Jackson was a senior. Auburn found teams could limit where Bo ran if he lined up as a halfback in the wishbone.

The I-formation is synonymous with the great University of Southern California teams and their tailbacks—Mike Garrett, O.J. Simpson, Anthony Davis, Charles White, Ricky Bell, and Marcus Allen. The formation's primary advantage is found in these names; it highlights the skills of sensational running backs.

The "I" also allows an offense to play power football, with the fullback blocking and leading the ball-carrier through the hole. In addition, the I-formation offers more versatility in play selection than some formations.

Split-Back Veer

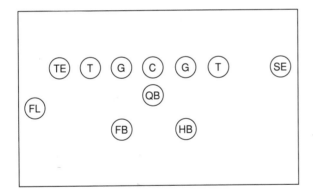

Bill Yoeman developed this formation at the University of Houston during the '60s and '70s. The split-back veer shares many principles, such as the hard halfback dive and the option, with Bud Wilkinson's Oklahoma Split-T of the '50s.

This formation's advantage is that it makes the most out of great speed in the backfield. The split-back veer is ideal for quick-hitting dives. It's also a good formation for spreading the defense, allowing you to run the option, and perhaps break a big play.

The split-back veer has weaknesses. It does not allow for much misdirection, and because of its spread, there is little opportunity for a power game out of this alignment.

Wing-T

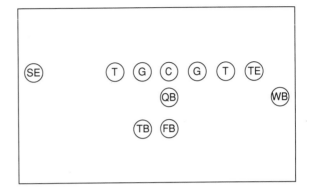

When you think of the Wing-T you immediately think of Dave Nelson, Forest Evashevski, and the University of Delaware. This formation has fallen out of fashion in *major* college football, but as I'll show later in this chapter, it can be adapted to emphasize its virtues and minimize its faults.

The Wing-T, like the old split-T and more recently the split-back veer, was designed to take advantage of team speed. In addition, because of the three-running-back set, the offense had the opportunity to use the speed of the dive, the power of the lead or trap, and the deception of the misdirected counter play.

Three Types of Running Plays

Before we get into specific plays from specific formations, I want to point out a few more elements of the running game. No matter what formation you're in or what terminology you use, you have three basic types of running plays from which to choose:

- Speed plays, such as the quick drive
- Power plays involving a lead block through the hole
- Deception plays, such as the counter or the reverse

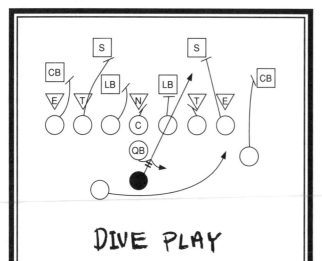

DIVE PLAY

When you have quick and fast runners and blockers it makes sense to use running plays that maximize their speed. One of the most basic speed plays is a hard dive by the fullback. On this play, the quarterback takes the ball from center, quickly pivots, and hands the ball to the fullback, who is running straight ahead at top speed. The offensive line also charges straight ahead at full speed.

The fullback dive is the speed play in the wishbone and the I-formation. From the veer and Wing-T, however, the fullback or halfback can run a speed play such as the hard dive. That's because both backs are an equal distance behind the line.

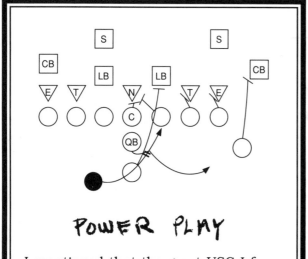

POWER PLAY

I mentioned that the great USC I-formation teams played power football. They played this style so effectively not because of their tremendous tailbacks but because of their All-American offensive linemen and their big blocking fullbacks.

When you say power play you are, in effect, saying "student-body right." Power plays involve a lead blocker back or a double-team block at the point of attack. The blocker functions like a snow plow, clearing a route for the ballcarrier to run through unimpeded.

In this example of a simple power play, the quarterback hands the ball off to the halfback, who follows the fullback's power lead block.

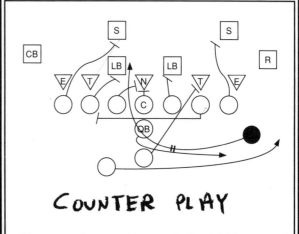

COUNTER PLAY

The speed game theory is that "They can't tackle what they can't catch." A variation of that approach says, "They can't tackle what they can't see." The third type of running play, the deception play, is based on that premise.

These plays try to fool the defense. Many deception plays include some element of misdirection: trying to get the defense to believe the play is going one way when it is really going the opposite way. A counter play is perhaps the most common example of a misdirection play.

In this counter play, the quarterback turns, and the flow of the play goes right. As the defense shifts to what it believes will be the point of attack, the quarterback hands the ball off to the halfback, who runs in the opposite direction—away from the flow.

Key

○ = Offensive player

▽ = Defensive lineman

□ = Defensive back

● = Offensive player to receive ball

‖ = Quarterback handoff

⟶ = Player movement

○—◁ = Offensive player blocking a defensive player

- - - - - = Pass

wwwww = Offensive player in motion before the snap

······· = Pitchout

THE MYTHICAL "BALANCED OFFENSE"

To me, the balanced attack is a myth. Statistics may show that you run the ball and you pass the ball for about the same number of yards, but to teach a truly balanced offensive attack is virtually impossible.

My reason for saying this is that I have seen no offensive line that could perform equally as well, consistently, on running plays and passing plays. To block well for the run, offensive linemen must be able to drive forward and make solid contact with their opponents across the line of scrimmage. Conversely, to pass block, your offensive linemen have to drop back a little, give up the line of scrimmage, and protect the passer. The two blocking techniques are entirely different.

So, when you talk or hear about a balanced offense, think again. Look at how well the line blocks on running plays versus passing plays, and draw your own conclusion.

Augustana Wing-T

Now I want to go into more depth and detail into a specific formation and the offensive system we've developed to run the ball from it. Because it is a unique system, we call it the Augustana Wing-T.

We developed this Wing-T version from the trap and misdirection principles of the Iowa or Delaware Wing-T and incorporated some of the speed and option principles of the Ohio State belly series of the same period, the late 1950s (see Figure 9.1a).

As a high school coach, I felt the Iowa Wing-T required too much blocking skill for the offensive guards and too much lateral movement for the backs. We wanted to go down the field, not sideline to sideline, and we wanted to use our best athletes (usually our backs) as both key blockers and runners.

The Augustana Wing-T formation is flexible; it can be run from a spread set (see Figure 9.1b), which is also an effective set from which to start power plays. It also lends itself to deceptive plays, which keep the defense honest.

From the Augustana Wing-T, we run four series of plays, demonstrating how multi-purpose this formation is for any team that emphasizes the run.

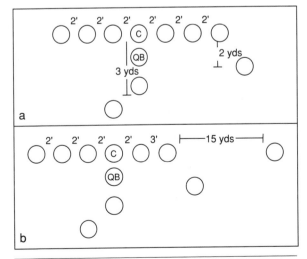

Figure 9.1 The Augustana Wing-T (a) from a tight set and (b) with the spread set.

Wing-T Series

The Wing-T series lets our offense spread the defense with the sweep—to power off-tackle like the single-wing and the misdirection of the counter play.

The series consists of three main plays:

FULLBACK DIVE—A speed play where the quarterback reverse pivots and hands to the fullback (see Figure 9.2a)

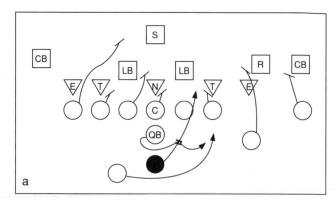

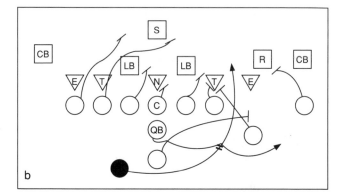

TAILBACK OFF-TACKLE—This is a combination of speed and power. The quarterback reverse pivots. The fullback comes toward the line and then moves parallel to it and toward the sideline. The quarterback continues behind the fullback and gives the ball to the tailback off-tackle (see Figure 9.2b).

WINGBACK COUNTER—This misdirection play begins with the same reverse pivot by the quarterback. The fullback moves forward and fills the hole (blocks) for the tackle, who is pulling. The tailback runs off-tackle, as on the previous play. The wingback, going opposite the flow but following the pulling tackle, takes the inside handoff from the quarterback (see Figure 9.2c).

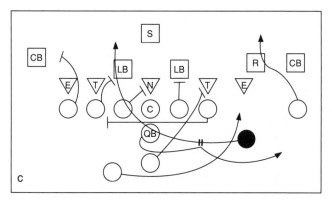

We also include a *toss sweep* in our Wing-T series (see Figure 9.2d). It is not a true series play, but we feel the need for the play to "stretch" the defense from our tight formation.

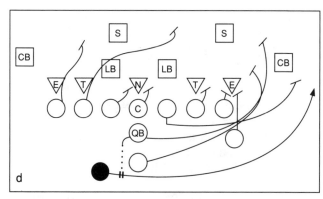

Figure 9.2 The four plays in the Wing-T series: (a) fullback dive, (b) tailback off-tackle, (c) wingback counter, and (d) toss sweep.

Inside Belly Series

The inside belly series gives our offense the speed and power of the fullback and the speed, power, and deception (created by the fullback belly fake) of our halfback off-tackle.

The inside belly series consists of two basic plays:

FULLBACK DIVE—A quickhitter begins the belly series. The quarterback turns immediately to the fullback side and hands the ball off to him immediately. The quarterback continues down the line as if he still has the ball and fakes a handoff to the wingback (see Figure 9.3a).

WINGBACK OPTION—This combines speed, power, and deception. It begins with the quarterback turning and placing the ball in the fullback's belly, faking the dive play. The quarterback pulls the ball out and continues down the line after the fullback clears. The wingback, who went into full-speed motion before the snap, takes the ball from the quarterback off-tackle (see Figure 9.3b).

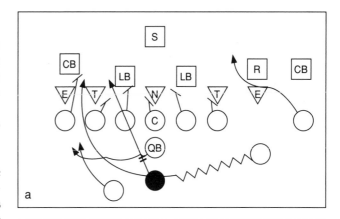

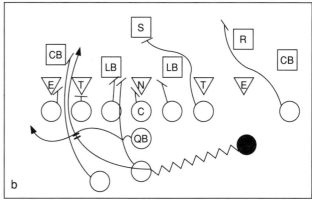

Figure 9.3 The two basic plays in the inside belly series: (a) fullback dive and (b) wingback option.

Outside Belly Series

The outside belly series is a variation of the inside belly options. It too combines speed, power, and deception plays. This is our triple option. The outside belly allows us to begin a play and have any one of three runners carry the ball—the fullback, the quarterback, or the wingback. It is truly an option.

The outside belly series has three primary options:

FULLBACK OFF-TACKLE—The quarterback turns at a 45-degree angle, places the ball in the fullback's belly, and steps forward with him to complete the handoff. The fullback runs hard and straight ahead with the ball (see Figure 9.4a). The quarterback continues down the line, faking as if he still has the ball. The wingback, who went into motion before the snap, stays deep as if preparing to receive a pitch.

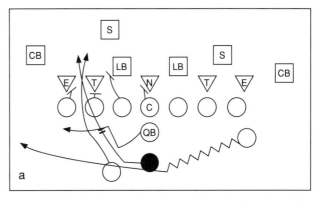

(continued)

Figure 9.4 The three primary options on the outside belly series: (a) fullback off-tackle, (b) quarterback option, and (c) wingback pitch.

QUARTERBACK OPTION—In this case, the quarterback pulls the ball out of the fullback's belly and continues down the line. He then reads that the defense's corner contain player has been blocked out of the play or is covering wide for a possible pitch to the tailback. The quarterback keeps the ball and runs for daylight (see Figure 9.4b).

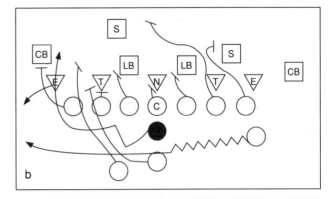

WINGBACK PITCH—When the fullback off-tackle and quarterback options are not available, the third alternative is for the quarterback to pitch to the wingback (see Figure 9.4c). The wingback must stay deep and wide enough and be at full speed when he receives the pitch.

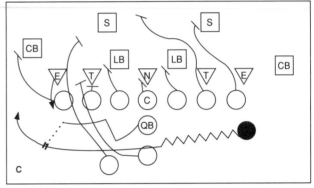

Figure 9.4 (continued) The three primary options on the outside belly series: (a) fullback off-tackle, (b) quarterback option, and (c) wingback pitch.

Trap Series

The trap series allows us to exploit (gap) defenses in which linemen are positioned between the players on our offensive front. It also incorporates power and deception. Many teams use the counter-trap option, which was made so famous during the '80s by the Washington Redskins.

The trap series includes two running plays with a bootleg option:

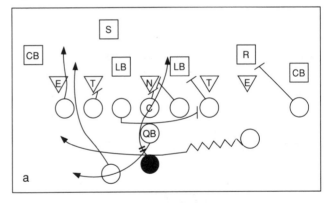

FULLBACK TRAP—The first option off this series begins with the quarterback turning, then stepping back almost as if he is getting ready to drop back or bootleg. The fullback goes right by the quarterback's hip, and follows the trap blocking up the middle (see Figure 9.5a). The quarterback then bootlegs as if he still has the ball. Note the halfback and tailback's roles.

COUNTER TRAP—This time the quarterback does not hand off to the fullback. Instead, he gives the ball to the halfback, then carries out his bootleg with the tailback trailing. The pulling guard and

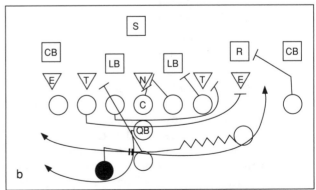

Figure 9.5 The two running plays off the trap series: (a) fullback trap and (b) counter trap.

tackle lead the halfback in the opposite direction (see Figure 9.5b).

Each play in the series is a set play with blocking adjustments designed to control the defense. The series or the option lets the offense take advantage of vulnerabilities in the defensive coverage and alignment.

Continuity

I remember looking through a book that claimed to include "the 99 best plays of the year." It had some great, innovative plays, all separate and different from one another.

In the real world, it doesn't work that way. You can neither teach 99 different running plays nor execute them against a defense.

As you can see from our four series of running plays, we believe it is important to have speed, power, and deception options in each of our attacks. We also believe that the *continuity* established by our four-series approach

- is easier to teach, which is especially helpful for inexperienced players;
- promotes precise execution because players do the same thing repeatedly;
- limits the types of blocks linemen are asked to make, increasing their ability to make the ones we need; and
- keeps the defense guessing because the formations and plays look the same.

That's a brief and general explanation of offensive continuity. Now let's look at a specific application of the concept from one of our 1985 playoff games.

Continuity in Action

In the first series of downs, we failed to gain a first down on two running plays and a swing pass. On our second possession we started at the 20-yard line, with 80 yards and a stiff defense between our offense and paydirt. The gusty wind in our face made the goal line seem even farther.

We continued our Wing-T Series, running our All-American halfback, Brad Price, off-tackle on first and second down. Brad's two runs totalled only a few yards. And on both runs we noted that the inside linebackers were keying on him (see Figure 9.6).

So on third and seven, we ran a counter

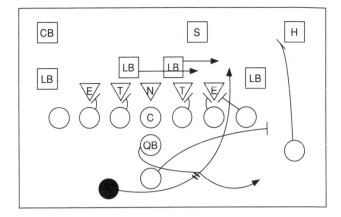

Figure 9.6   An off-tackle power play.

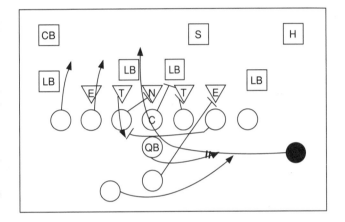

Figure 9.7   A counter play.

play that looks very similar to our off-tackle option in the series, except in this case our wingback takes the handoff running opposite the flow of the other offensive backs (see Figure 9.7). With the inside linebackers keying on Price, our wingback ran for a big gain and a first down.

After that counter play, the linebackers weren't quite so quick to flow with the movements of our fullback and halfback. As a result, we began chewing up yards at three and four yards a clip, never trying to pass against the wind. We scored a touchdown to end the drive, having maintained possession for nearly the whole quarter.

Coaching Tips for the Running Game

People always ask coaches whose teams successfully run the football what their "secret" is. We have no secrets. What you've read in this chapter is what we do.

However, here are six suggestions that will help you get the kind of performance you seek from your running game:

_____

Tip #1:

Make your system broad enough to take advantage of what the defense will allow. For example, if you can see that the linebackers are flowing very fast in one direction, you need the counter or counter trap in your arsenal.

Tip #2:

Understand the duties of each position—running, blocking, faking—and place your players in the positions that optimize their talents.

Tip #3:

This is related to Tip #2. Evaluate your runners. Make the most of their skills by placing them in the best position in the best formation possible on each play. If you have a great speed back, you want to line him up so that he gets the ball on plays designed to outrun the defense.

Tip #4:

Decide whether to do a few things very well or a lot of things not so well. Keep your plays simple enough to teach to your players within their concentration time frame.

Tip #5:

Design a system that lets you adjust during the game and that will not confuse your players. The four series we use are similar enough that players readily make the changes we ask of them.

Tip #6:

You will play as you practice. To execute any run offense, you must repeat and repeat the plays you intend to use. Some plays require that you practice full speed and with live contact.

_____

Summary

Here are the main points discussed in this chapter on the running game:

1. A formation is not an offense. Run formations simply position your offense so it can best execute plays against the defense.
2. Running plays may be designed to highlight speed, power, or deception, but few plays offer all three.
3. The run formation you choose should be the best alignment for the type of play you have in mind.
4. Whatever system you select for running the football, make sure you know it thoroughly and can teach it to players.
5. If your run offense has continuity, you'll be a lot tougher to defend. Continuity allows you to take advantage of what the defense gives you.

Chapter 10

Teaching the Passing Game

Because we are a run-first football team, some people jump to the conclusion that we're also a no-pass football team. Not true. In fact, during my first year at Augustana when our players were more suited for the passing game, we led our conference in passing.

Some say that "If you stop Augie on the ground, you've got 'em." Perhaps those people forget that Eric Welgat, a fine receiver for us, set an NCAA Division III playoff record with the most receiving yards in a single game. As all teams, we need the ability to pass well.

Yes, we emphasize the run for all the reasons stated in chapter 9. But we know the pass is important to complement our running game and to highlight our players' strengths.

Establishing a Passing Game

A good offensive football team must have the *ability* both to run and to pass. That does not mean a good offensive team must run and pass an equal number of times.

You need the pass for the big-play threat, to get the long first downs, and to move the ball quickly at the end of the half or game.

If you are a threat to pass, the defense can't stack the line of scrimmage. And by spreading the defense, you open up the running game.

 A SIMPLE SOLUTION

In our 1984 NCAA quarterfinal game, we were pitted against a Dayton team that everyone presumed would be our biggest obstacle against repeating as national champions. As usual, we had emphasized the running game on our way to an undefeated regular season.

Our passing game was not very sophisticated. In fact, during the game I called our sophomore quarterback (Kirk Bednar) and our best receiver (Norm Singbush) over to the sideline and asked the receiver if he was open on most of his routes. He said he was, so I directed our quarterback to drop back and throw it to him. The quarterback did and threw 12 completions to the one receiver. We won the game 14-13. In this case, with a young quarterback and a great receiver, the simpler the better.

A good running game also enhances the passing game. Many run-oriented offenses incorporate short passes and passes that call for a quick, three-step quarterback drop and little change in blocking schemes. And if you run the ball well enough, play-action passes are usually effective because the defense must respect the fake.

Three Types of Pass Plays

Because we are primarily a running team, we developed into a selective passing team. We try to incorporate all three types of pass plays to complement our running game.

Timed Passes

The timing pattern involves two elements. First, the quarterback takes a 3-, 5-, or 7-step straight drop. Second, the quarterback and receivers synchronize the last step of the quarterback's drop with the receiver's break and look for the ball.

The quarterback throws the ball to a spot where the receiver will be, not where the receiver is when the ball is released. On longer patterns, the quarterback needs a deeper pocket and needs to lead the receiver more with the ball.

Figure 10.1 illustrates a typical timed pass play. The three routes shown—the drag, flag,

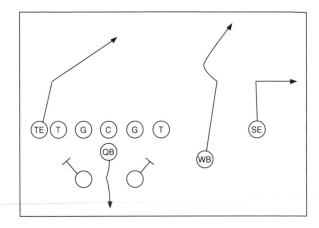

Figure 10.1　A typical timed pass play.

and square cut—are commonly used for timed patterns.

Tall, strong-armed quarterbacks typically execute these plays best. They have the height to look over the top of the defense, and can put necessary zip on the ball to complete passes before the defense reacts.

Sprint-Out and Bootleg Passes

In this age of the mobile quarterback, many coaches favor the sprint-out or bootleg play. These plays offer a moving pocket, a great advantage to smaller, quicker quarterbacks. And because the pocket is moving, it is more difficult for the defense to sack the quarterback.

Although usually effective, the sprint-out pass has drawbacks: The quarterback must always remember to square up to the target (receiver or spot) when he throws; poor throwing habits can develop from throwing on the move, and few quarterbacks throw as well sprinting in the direction opposite their throwing arm.

In addition, sprint-out and bootleg passes allow the defense to cover only half the field. It is almost impossible to throw the ball all the way back across the field from a sprint in the opposite direction. Note that in Figure 10.2 all potential receivers are to the right of the center when the quarterback reaches throwing position.

Play-Action Passes

Good running teams often like to throw after faking one of their successful running plays.

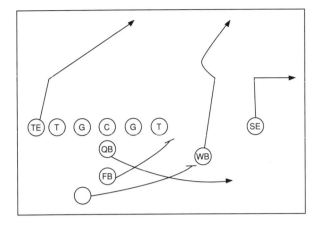

Figure 10.2 The sprint-out or bootleg pass.

The reason is apparent: The defense must respect and play the run, which makes it more likely the offense can spring open a receiver. In addition, the run fake freezes the defensive line, giving the quarterback more time to throw.

The example (see Figure 10.3) shows the quarterback reverse pivoting and faking the handoff to the fullback. After the fake, the quarterback takes a few more steps, sets, and throws. If the defensive backs creep up to stop what they think is a running play, the receiver will be open.

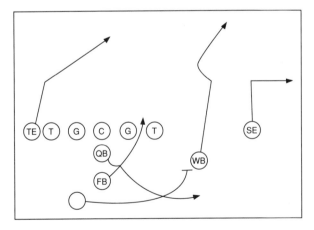

Figure 10.3 A play-action pass: The quarterback reverse pivots and fakes the handoff to the fullback.

Passing Tree

All three types of pass plays include routes off of a "passing tree"—the basic pass pat-

terns receivers will run within an offense. Those five routes are illustrated in Figure 10.4.

1. *Square out*—Receiver sprints off line, plants hard, runs a 90-degree-angle to sideline at 5, 7, or 10 yards.
2. *Flag*—Receiver sprints off line, fakes to inside, and runs a 45-degree-angle route toward the sideline.
3. *Take off*—Receiver sprints toward goal and looks over inside shoulder.
4. *Post*—Opposite of flag route. Receiver runs 45-degree-angle to goal post or center of field.
5. *Curl*—Receiver sprints off line of scrimmage and curls or settles into a vacant area on field at 8, 10, or 12 yards.

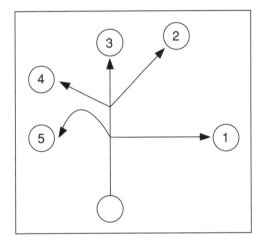

Figure 10.4 The five routes of the passing tree.

Receivers, of course, run many more pass routes than are represented on the passing tree. So why have it? Why teach it to your players?

The best reason is that it gives them enough different pass routes to keep the defense guessing but a reasonable number for even inexperienced players to learn well.

The passing tree also structures a pass offense. Instead of running helter-skelter all over the field, players run disciplined pass routes, which helps a quarterback anticipate receivers' moves and where to spot the ball.

Finally, by coordinating passing tree routes, the offense can spread the defense.

One safety can't guard two receivers because the receivers aren't bunched together on the field. If you have an exceptional receiver, the defense must decide whether to double-team, zone, or hope that one player can hold his own in isolation. If the defense chooses to go one-on-one, the offense is just one minor error from scoring.

Once receivers learn the passing tree, they can incorporate these routes into any offensive formation or system. For example, from the pro formation in a pass-oriented offense, receivers might run timing patterns as shown in Figure 10.5.

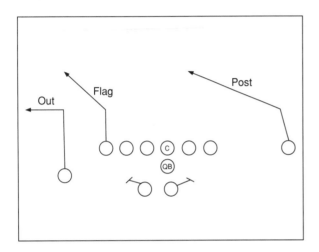

Figure 10.5 Timing patterns from the pro formation.

We use the passing tree on play-action passes to teach the receivers their routes. But a play-action pass is like an assigned play: The routes are constant and are arranged to take advantage of an overanxious secondary. The run fake is the key to this play more than the receivers' exact pass routes.

Selecting a Pass Formation

A pass offense, like a run offense, starts with a formation. The pass formation you select should maximize your players' ability and take advantage of the defense.

Pass formations usually try to isolate one or more receivers away from defensive help

and make it harder for the defense to detain receivers at the line of scrimmage. That's why the formations you'll see next differ so much from the run formations in chapter 9.

Pro Set

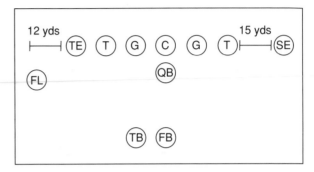

For years, teams committed to the passing game preferred the pro set as their base formation. It allows for two wide-outs—a split end and a flanker. The pro set also uses a tight end, a strong player who can either block for the run or catch short passes and then run with the ball when he hauls it in. The formation is designed to make ultimate use of both running backs, who are threats to run or to catch short flare passes in the flats.

The classic quarterback in this type of formation, someone like Joe Namath or Dan Marino, prefers to take the straight drop and throw deep. The shotgun formation achieves the same passing position, without requiring the quarterback drop (see Figure 10.6). The shotgun is somewhat riskier because it requires a 5-yard center snap, but it gives the

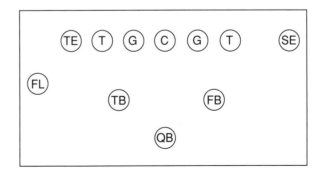

Figure 10.6 The shotgun formation.

quarterback a better and longer look at the defensive pass rush and coverage than does the pro set. The shotgun offers fewer run options.

One-Back Formation

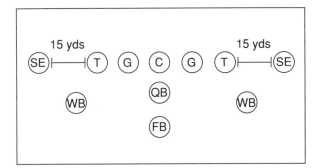

A good example of a formation getting confused with an offense is the one-back formation and the run-and-shoot offense. Many teams have used the single-back alignment for various offensive purposes. Conversely, the run-and-shoot (originally devised by Tiger Ellison in the '60s) is run to stretch the defense. It was no accident that the Detroit Lions, when committed to the run-and-shoot under offensive coordinator June Jones, called the offense the "Silver Stretch."

If you run an offense from a single-back formation, you need an outstanding running back and a corps of excellent receivers. A great pass-blocking line helps too. The Washington Redskins have had all three during the '80s and early '90s, with Riggins at H-back; Art Monk, Gary Clark, and Ricky Sanders at receiver; and the "Hogs" up front.

Because the one-back formation spreads more people along the line of scrimmage, the defense is forced to stretch horizontally—one sideline to the other. And because the offense poses a greater deep threat, the defense must stretch vertically—line of scrimmage to goal line.

Unless you have a sensational running back, like a Barry Sanders, you are not likely to run the ball effectively from the one-back set: You have one fewer blocking back and one fewer blocker up front (tight end). That is why the run-and-shoot formation is known as a passing offense.

Base Formation

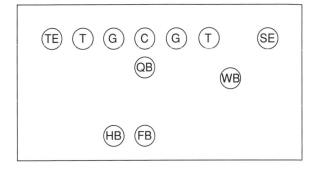

If your passing game emphasizes play-action passes, you'll usually line up in running formation. Remember, the key to play action passes working is getting the defense to believe you are running the football. So, position the line and backfield the same before a play-action pass play as before a run.

It works the other way too. If you present a threat to pass, in your base formation, the defense cannot overplay the run.

Passing at Augustana

Some might jest that this section's title is an oxymoron. But we really do throw the football, and we do use more than our base formation in our passing game.

Because we usually run the football effectively, we try to use that to our advantage on most pass plays. Many of our opponents focus their defensive strategy on stopping the run. They stack the line, especially in the middle, and bring their defensive backs closer to the line of scrimmage. That doesn't stop us from running, but it does provide good passing opportunities. And we've had the most success passing when we fake one of our better running plays and our receivers get a step on their defender, who overplayed the run. So most of our passes are play-action and are thrown from our base formation—the Augustana Wing-T.

Next is a sampling of our pass plays. Notice that our receivers have assigned routes on each play. Also see that our quarterback drops back, sprints out, bootlegs, or fakes the run, depending on the needs of a specific pass play.

Receiver Numbering System

At Augustana we number our receivers as follows:

① = split end (or the end on the side of the wingback)

② = tailback

③ = fullback

④ = wingback (or flanker in pro set)

⑨ = tight end

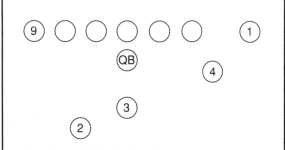

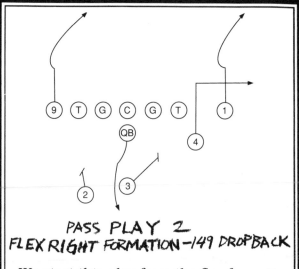

PASS PLAY 2
FLEX RIGHT FORMATION –149 DROPBACK

We start this play from the flex formation with the split end on the wing's side. The quarterback takes a quick 3- or 5-step straight drop and looks right, for either the split end running a flag or the wingback running an out pattern. If the defense has both receivers covered, the quarterback checks the middle of the field for the tight end running a post pattern.

This play tries to force one-on-one coverage on the tight end over the middle.

Wing-T Series

The success of play-action passes is determined by the strength of your running game and your offense's execution of the plays you call. For example, if you're gaining very little yardage on quick-hitting, inside running plays, the opponent's defensive backs will feel less responsible for stopping the run (their teammates up front are stopping it without assistance). The backs, then, will be less likely to bite when the quarterback fakes a handoff. And, if the quarterback fakes poorly, the defensive backs will be less prone to get tricked out of good pass coverage position, even if your offense has been running the ball effectively.

We run the next four play-action passes, including the fake fullback dive play, from our Wing-T formation. These are typically some of our most successful running plays, so we often catch the defensive secondary overcommitting to stop the run, taking the quarterback's fake and coming up too quickly to stuff what they think is a running play, or positioning too many players at the line so that their coverage is inadequate.

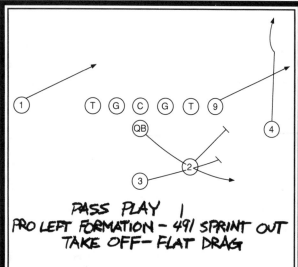

PASS PLAY 1
PRO LEFT FORMATION – 491 SPRINT OUT
TAKE OFF– FLAT DRAG

From the pro set, we have the quarterback sprint right, and we flood that side of the field with receivers. The split end drags across, the wingback runs a take-off route, and the tight end runs a flat pattern to the sideline. This play is especially effective when the flat is open because of the strong safety's position.

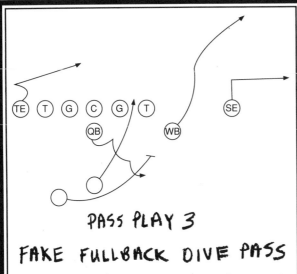

PASS PLAY 3
FAKE FULLBACK DIVE PASS

The quarterback, after a good fake to the fullback, looks for an open receiver on the right side of the field. If the fake causes the strong safety to sneak up, the wingback may be open over the top on a flag pattern.

This is a good play to use when you are running strong up the middle and when defensive backs are overplaying the run.

This is a great play to use when the linebackers are reacting quickly to stop the fullback. The tight end should be open in the seam between the linebacker and the safety.

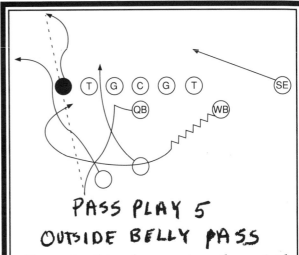

PASS PLAY 5
OUTSIDE BELLY PASS

To work, this play requires the outside belly option threat. If the cornerback comes up too hard to tackle the pitchman (wingback), the quarterback has an open tight end to throw to 10 or 15 yards downfield. If the cornerback hangs deep with the tight end, the halfback in the flat should be open. Obviously, this play is going to work best when you are running the ball well with the outside belly series. You must set up this pass by the run on the scouting report.

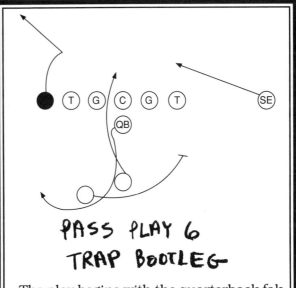

PASS PLAY 4
PASS OFF INSIDE BELLY SERIES

This is a quick-hitting play-action pass from our inside belly series. After faking to the fullback, the quarterback comes to an immediate stop and fires to the tight end, who is running a "look" route where he simply looks for the ball after releasing from the line of scrimmage. A key to this play is for the quarterback to keep the ball, which is thrown low, from being batted down. Also, the tight end cannot get tied up at the line of scrimmage.

PASS PLAY 6
TRAP BOOTLEG

The play begins with the quarterback faking the fullback trap and getting the defense to flow with the backfield action. After the fake, the quarterback bootlegs away from the flow and looks for the tight end, who runs a short flag route.

The trap bootleg is especially effective against defensive secondaries that quickly rotate their coverage areas.

Coaching Tips for the Passing Game

Like running, passing the football has become option football to a degree: Take what the defense allows. If the defense is deep, pass short. If the defense is tight and aggressive, try for the home run.

The pass offense also needs to use your players' strengths wisely. If you use a split end, find one that is good enough to command respect—such as double coverage—from the defense.

Another aspect of the running game that applies to the passing game is that you must practice over and over. And you must practice the pass *under pressure*. Don't just let your quarterback and receivers play catch when you work on your pass plays. They need to get their timing down going full speed against a defense. Action passes are memorized pass patterns to take advantage of the defense. The receivers must know their routes when the play is called.

Summary

The passing game can be a great asset to any offense. Here are the things to remember about your passing attack:

1. To be a good offensive team you must be able to pass the football effectively.
2. Use pass formations to enhance your players' strengths and offensive system.
3. If you choose to be a pass-first team, study it, practice it, and teach it well enough so that you can balance your passing game with the run.
4. Passing the football is no easier than running it. So emphasize hard, full-speed practice as the way to make the pass offense click.

Part IV

Coaching Defense

Chapter 11

Basic Defensive Positions and Alignments

Championships are won with great defense.

True, the offense gets most of the glamour. But glamour doesn't keep an opponent from marching down the field in the fourth quarter.

Our players often repeat the slogan "Offense is the show, but defense is the key." More simply they say, " 'O' is the show, and 'D' is the key." Our coaching staff believe that. But more importantly, our players believe it.

Because everyone in our program greatly values the defense, our players compete

fiercely for each defensive position. This raises the performance level of defensive players—starters and nonstarters.

Odd vs. Even Defenses

Unlike offenses, defenses aren't required to have a minimum number of players on the line of scrimmage. Therefore, you can line up a defense in almost any arrangement.

Actually, there are two types of defensive alignments, distinguished by whether the defense positions a lineman directly across from the offensive center. A defense that covers the center is called an odd defense, and typically has five linemen (see Figure 11.1).

When the defense does not cover the center, it is called an even defense. In this case, the line is usually four players strong (see Figure 11.2).

Whether you choose the odd or even defensive alignment, you'll have players at these three positions: defensive lineman, linebacker, and defensive back.

Defensive Linemen

When you determine whether linemen will play offense or defense, use these rules of thumb: Size is more important on the offensive line; speed is more important on the defensive front. Put simply, defensive linemen can't hit them if they can't catch them.

Most people look for big defensive linemen. But it is even more important for defensive linemen to have the ability and quickness to make contact, separate from the offense, and run to the football.

How you position your defensive line should take advantage of the system and your personnel.

Noseguard

If you play an odd defense, you must have your best lineman at noseguard. And if you have an outstanding noseguard, you probably have an outstanding defense. In 1986, when Augustana led the nation in defense, it was no coincidence that the defense was anchored by an All-American noseguard, Brian King.

A good noseguard helps keep blockers off the linebackers by occupying the center and the two guards. Because he is in the center of the formation, the noseguard has the most opportunities to disrupt the offense and to get to the football.

Noseguards are usually short, with low centers of gravity. Starting each play from a low, four-point stance, noseguards must prevent linemen from knocking them off their feet. Noseguards need to be quick so they can get off the ball in an instant. Finally, noseguards need to be tenacious. Double-teams can't discourage them. Second and third efforts are habits.

Tackles

Often bigger than the noseguard, defensive tackles are the anchors, the front wall that

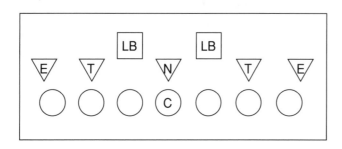

N=Nose tackle
T=Tackle
E=Defensive end
LB=Linebacker
CB=Cornerback
S=Safety
R=Rover
H=Halfback

Figure 11.1 An odd defense covers the center and typically has five linemen.

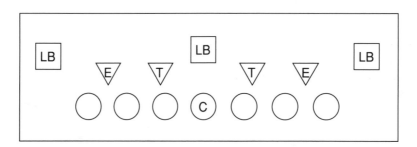

Figure 11.2 An even defense does not cover the center and usually has four linemen.

prevents the offense from running over the defense. Tackles must occupy blockers so that inside linebackers are free to track down the football.

Ideally, defensive tackles will be able to penetrate the offensive line and disrupt running and pass plays. Against drop-back passing teams, a good defensive tackle will help break down the pocket and hurry or sack the quarterback. We once had such a defensive tackle, Lynn Thomsen, who started all 50 games during his career. It's no coincidence that we won all 50.

Ends

Taller and more agile than other defensive linemen, defensive ends are now much like linebackers. In fact, starting from their two-point stance, today's defensive ends look very much like yesterday's outside linebackers. The prototype of this end-linebacker combination was Ted Hendricks, who played for the Colts and Raiders. More recently, teams are using what they call a "rush linebacker," who often plays the role of a blitzing defensive end.

Defensive ends must be strong enough to take on pulling linemen, tight ends, and fullbacks. They must be quick enough to rush the passer and cover backs out in the flats. And they must be smart enough to read deception plays like end-arounds, counters, screens, and play-action passes. In short, they need to be more athletic than other linemen.

Linebackers

Inside linebackers are the heart of any great defense, especially a run defense. They must possess quickness, instinct, and aggressiveness.

Because linebackers are positioned away from the line, they are free to move before being blocked. Inside linebackers should be strong enough to take on interior offensive linemen and fullbacks straight up. Outside linebackers must be fast enough and athletic enough to cover the open field and contain runners and receivers.

Defensive Backs

No matter your system, your defensive backs should be the most skilled athletes on the team. When I started coaching, I used to look for my cornerbacks and safeties on the basketball courts—guys who could outsprint, outrebound, and beat others to the ball. That's the kind of player you need to cover the opponent's best athletes—wide receivers.

The free safety watches the offense's play begin to develop, then reacts in the direction of the ball. In contrast, the strong safety aggressively attacks the ball, similar to a linebacker. The strong safety is the defensive back most responsible for supporting the run defense.

The defensive backfield is not a place for the faint of heart. One slip by a defensive back means 6 points. That may be true at other positions, but the defensive back who slips up is on display for everyone to see. There's nowhere to hide when you miss a tackle in the open field or let a receiver get free for a touchdown.

Choosing a Defensive Formation

The defensive formation you select, like your offensive formation, should be the best alignment for your system and your personnel. An additional concern for defensive formations is how well they cover the field against the offense.

Just as in baseball—where fielders are positioned to take away hitters' strengths so that no one bats .400—football coaches use the boundaries and the placement of players to minimize the probability of success by the offense. Here are three basic defensive alignments and a summary of their strengths and weaknesses.

The 5-2

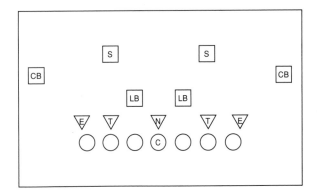

This is what the pros call a 3-4 defense. At the high school and college levels, we count the defensive ends as linemen; the pros count what are essentially the same players as linebackers.

The 5-2, an odd defense with a four-deep secondary, offers maximum pass coverage and still provides run support from the extra defensive back. Therefore, it's a good formation to use if you have a noseguard and want a four-deep secondary.

The disadvantage of the 5-2 alignment is that you need three good down linemen and a strong cornerback.

The 4-3

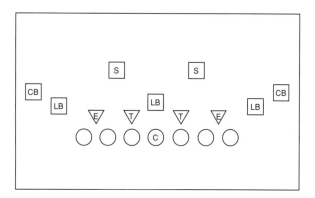

This is the standard pro alignment, with big defensive ends and no noseguard. The outside linebackers have to be versatile enough to fight off blocks from tight ends and fullbacks and fast enough to cover backs on pass routes. Again, the standard four-deep secondary is used.

The 4-3's advantages are that you have four big men to help with the run and one outstanding middle linebacker who is free to go to the ball.

This formation's disadvantage is the need for a great middle linebacker who takes the place of the "2" in the 5-2.

The 4-4, or Split 6

This formation is much like the 4-3, except one safety position is converted into an inside linebacker. Note also that the inside linebackers line up behind the tackles.

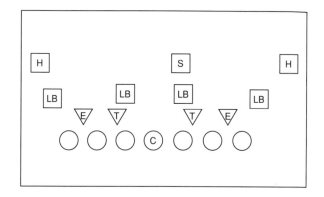

The 4-4 is ideal for a big defense playing teams that emphasize the run. With so much manpower at the line of scrimmage, the 4-4 is especially strong against the run. When you play a team with little ability or inclination to pass, this is a defense worth considering. It is also an option in short-yardage situations.

The formation's obvious drawback is its inability to handle pass-oriented offenses. How do you counter a one-back offensive set and cover a speedy wingback with a slow-footed linebacker? And in zone coverage, think of the gaping holes an accurate quarterback would exploit.

Augustana Defense

At Augustana we choose to align our defense from a standard 5-2 formation. With the four-deep secondary, we use a strong safety to aid with the run. We believe this formation best fits our players' skills and that it stacks up well against most offenses on our schedule.

We started using this basic alignment in high school, after many years of using an even 4-4 (or Split 6) formation. Here's why we switched.

    TIME TO SWITCH

Throughout the '60s and early '70s, we were a good defensive team, shutting out about half the teams on our schedule. But when the state playoff system began in 1974, we found that to compete against Illinois' best teams we needed more run support from the secondary and more ability to cover the pass formation. About the same time, we had a linebacker who was not disciplined enough to play that position but who could become a great noseguard.

So in 1976 we switched from a 4-4 to a 5-2. We won the state championship that year, and the noseguard made the All-State team.

At Augustana, as in high school, we interchange (flip-flop) our two deep backs. Our strong safety (whom we call our rover) always teams up with one cornerback (whom we call our halfback); opposite these two is our cornerback. The free safety will be in the middle.

The rover and halfback usually play the wide side of the field or the strength of the formation, unless the scouting report suggests otherwise.

By naming and pairing these deep backs, we take advantage of individual skills. We hope the rover and halfback complement each other to form a tough twosome. Because we cannot give scholarships to blue chippers for each position, it is critical that players' talents be well distributed in our defensive alignment.

Good defensive linemen are basic to the 5-2. We need strong athletes at the noseguard and the tackles.

Summary

1. There are three distinct defensive positions: linemen (noseguard, tackles, and ends); linebackers (inside and outside); and backs (strong safety, free safety, and cornerbacks).
2. The defensive line forces the offense to hurry on pass plays and to hesitate or run wide on running plays.
3. The linebackers and ends react to and contain the counterforce applied by the offense.
4. The deep backs are and must be the most skilled because one mistake can cost you 6 points.
5. Align your defense to give your players the best chance. Nobody should hit .400 against you.
6. Recognize when a change of formation is needed, and consider all the pluses and minuses of alternative formations.

Chapter 12

Teaching Defensive Skills

Each of the three general defensive positions—lineman, linebacker, and back—must be filled by players with specialized skills. Defensive players, like offensive players, require position-specific techniques.

But there is one skill every defender must perform well: tackling. A defensive player may be strong, fast, quick, and have all kinds of other talents, but if he can't tackle, he can't play. To emphasize the importance of this skill to you and to encourage you to share that emphasis with your players, I'm leading off this chapter with a section on teaching tackling.

Tackling

A good tackler has his knees bent, his head up, and his eyes focused on the football. I tell players to center on the football because then they'll place the head in front of the ballcarrier's body. By keeping his eyes on the ball, the defender also keeps his head up and his helmet back and doesn't strike the runner with the helmet first.

A player should *never* use the helmet as a weapon. It is a hard and dangerous piece of equipment. And it's self-destructive for the defender: It's probably more dangerous to the tackler than to the ballcarrier because the defender has his neck exposed if his helmet is down.

In addition to focusing on the ball, teach defensive players to explode *through* the ballcarrier. The tackler should keep his legs moving and drive his hips to the ground so that he can lift as he wraps his arms around the runner. A defender's powerful arm action is important so that the ballcarrier can't bounce off the initial hit.

In short, teach defenders this basic tackling technique: focus eyes on ball, drive legs and accelerate through the runner, lift and wrap strongly. Then have players practice this skill repeatedly through drills and scrimmages.

Tackling Drill

One-on-One Tackling Drill

Purpose. To teach the fundamentals of a good head-on tackle against a runner, not a sled

Procedure.   Line a 5-yard square in paint. One player, the ballcarrier, stands on one corner, while the other player positions himself on the opposite, diagonal corner. The ballcarrier runs *straight up*, full speed toward the tackler (not over the tackler—this is a tackling drill). The tackler makes the tackle with his head up and his eyes on the ball, driving his legs, wrapping his arms around the ballcarrier, and taking him to the ground.

Coaching Points.   Check all fundamentals. The short distance between the players at the start reduces the chance of injury but improves the chance for the perfect tackle. This drill also can be used for angle tackling. Be sure the ballcarrier runs down the line. Emphasize keeping the eyes on the ball and holding the ball away from the tackler.

Defensive Linemen

The defensive lineman's stance must allow him to move quickly, deliver a blow, and run. It is slightly different than an offensive lineman's stance: A defensive lineman can "tilt" or angle to gain advantage.

Defensive linemen must fight off blockers on every play, so they need a variety of skills for handling their position. The four basic techniques that all defensive linemen should know are the *read*, *pressure*, *slant*, and *swim*.

In the "read," the defensive man delivers a blow to the offensive lineman with the forearm or hands and then separates and runs to the football. (If you use the hands, try to get inside leverage on the offense.) Emphasize that the first blow the lineman applies to the blocker is the most important fundamental because it allows the player to neutralize the offensive charge.

When splitting the gap to pressure the offense, the defensive lineman must drive low and hard between the offensive linemen. The lineman's objective here is to penetrate the offense so he can get behind the line of scrimmage and into the backfield.

In a slant technique, the defensive man is usually lined head up on (directly across from) the offensive lineman. The defender's first movement must be a quick crossover step, combined with a rip (in which he throws his inside arm through the arms of the blocker) to get by the opponent and into a gap. This move tends to stop an offensive lineman's charge because he has a smaller target.

The swim technique is used on an opponent who is head up. The swim requires the defensive man to strike the opponent's left forearm with his right hand, keeping the blocker from moving laterally. Simultaneously, the defensive lineman must swim his left arm over the top of the opponent's helmet and use that arm as a barrier to push by the out-of-position offensive lineman.

Defensive Line Drill

Slant and Run

Purpose.   To teach the slant technique and quick reaction after it

Procedure.   Defensive lineman head up on offensive lineman. On the snap of the ball, the defensive player quickly crosses over, rips the offensive lineman, then squares up in the hole. After squaring, the lineman sprints forward.

Coaching Points.   Check the quickness of the defensive player's first move and how much authority he has in his rip. Make sure he has these first two moves mastered; he won't have a chance to square up and sprint if he doesn't.

Linebackers

Linebackers start each play from a standing position, knees bent, feet as wide apart as their shoulders, head up, back straight, and arms down ready to deliver a blow or fend off blockers. This stance provides a solid base from which to move and to see the offense.

The fundamental rule for linebackers is *never to give ground.* Linebackers must move quickly and powerfully and react instinctively to the play.

However, a good linebacker doesn't get by on innate ability alone. Help your linebackers by identifying offensive keys to which they should respond. Some defensive schemes key on guards, some key on the running backs, and some key on the quarterback.

These keys aid the linebacker's reaction. But being smart does not substitute for being sound in technique and tough. Even if the linebacker gets in good position to stop the play, he must be able to take on the charging block, deliver a blow with a short step, and make a stand.

The following drills are the best to teach those techniques.

Linebacker Drills

In the Box

Purpose.   To teach linebackers to deliver a blow with one short step and not to give ground

Procedure.   Mark a 2-yard square. Position a linebacker in the box. Have two or three linemen line up 5 yards from the linebacker. On command, the linemen try to block the linebacker out of the box. One blocker is quickly followed by a second (see Figure 12.1).

Coaching Points.   Check to see that the linebacker gets a good base, keeps his head up, and delivers a strong blow to get rid of each block attempt. Provide rapid instruction throughout this drill, reminding the linebacker about proper technique.

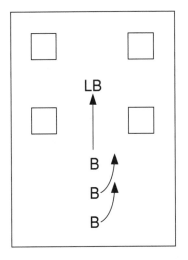

Figure 12.1   In-the-box linebacker drill.

Step Into the Hole

Purpose.   To teach linebackers to flow to the ball and to come forward for the tackle

Procedure.   Line up hard dummies across the field to simulate an offensive front. Use a ballcarrier and a linebacker to mirror each other on both sides of the line of dummies. The ballcarrier runs laterally and comes forward into a gap. The linebacker mirrors the runner and comes into the gap to make the tackle (see Figure 12.2).

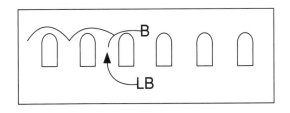

Figure 12.2   Step-into-the-hole linebacker drill.

Coaching Points. Focus on good stance—a low, quick move so that the linebacker can deliver the tackle while going forward.

Defensive Backs

Teaching defensive back techniques is much the same as teaching one-on-one defensive fundamentals to basketball players. You must teach the back to line up, with knees bent, ready to backpedal or turn and run with the receiver.

When defending man-to-man against a receiver, backs should always allow a 2- to 3-yard cushion and center in on the receiver's belt buckle. In the one-on-one situation, the receiver must be the defensive back's focus, shadowing him all over the field. Footwork, quickness, agility, and speed are essential.

When the defense is in zone coverage, backs don't play receivers so tight. Instead, they focus on the quarterback's eyes and protect a designated area of the field.

Defensive backs—especially safeties—also must know how to play the run. Teach them to come up strong once the offense commits to a running play; then to stop, plant, and attack the ballcarrier. Like linebackers, defensive backs need a nose for the ball. And, although you hope it never comes to this, speedy defensive backs can run down offensive players who have broken free for apparent touchdowns.

The variety of physical demands that defensive backs face shows why you should use your best athletes in those positions. If you do, you just might reduce points scored against you.

Defensive Back Drills

Protect the Zone

Purpose. To teach the defensive back that with the proper angle and fundamentals, he can outrun the football and cover a deep zone

Procedure. Line up receivers on both hash marks, with a defensive back in the middle of the field 5 yards off the line. While backpedaling to stay ahead of the receivers, the defensive back keeps his eyes on the quarterback. The quarterback turns to one side to throw. The defensive back reads the quarterback, rolls his hips, and sprints toward the intended receiver to intercept (see Figure 12.3).

Coaching Points. Your quarterback should throw high and deep—at least 25 yards downfield. Watch that the defensive backs take the proper angle to intercept the pass. They should not go flat toward the sidelines. Their reaction to the pass should be like a good outfielder who gets a great jump on the ball at the crack of the bat and runs to where the ball will drop.

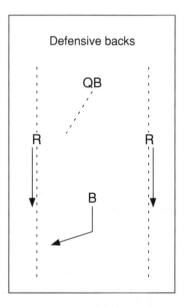

Figure 12.3 Protect-the-zone defensive back drill.

A second defensive back drill, Release, Go, Jump, Catch, is explained in chapter 8. Put a deep back on the receiver in bump-and-run man coverage and throw the ball. Instruct both offense and defense to go after the ball and not wait for it to come down.

Summary

1. Every good defensive player is a good tackler. Emphasize this skill to your defenders more than any other.
2. Defensive linemen must maximize their quickness. Teach them the read, pressure, slant, and swim techniques so they never should stay blocked.
3. Linebackers smell out the play and react. As the hub of the defense, linebackers should have the mindset and the tackling skills not to give the offense an inch.
4. Defensive backs are in a high-risk position. For insurance, put your most physically talented athletes at defensive back and teach them the pass and run defense techniques they need to succeed.

Chapter 13

Teaching Team Defense

Most coaches agree that a great defense is the key to a successful program. Defense gives you consistency and the chance to win, even if your offense sputters.

Actually, a great defense is the key to continued success in every sport. It's true that if you don't score, you don't win. But if you don't let your opponent score, you don't lose.

We've looked at each defensive position in isolation, but great defense is possible only if you coordinate your linemen, linebackers, and backs. This coordination of personnel includes positioning players effectively, complementing individual players' skills with their teammates' skills, and calling for defensive strategies that maximize the players' collective strengths.

In this chapter we'll look at the thinking that goes into developing a defensive scheme and how this approach should match with your offensive system. Then we'll examine what we at Augustana did to design a successful defense, and how we adjust formations, personnel, and strategies during games.

Choosing Your Defensive Approach

The strongest defenses, like great offenses, are one-dimensional. By that I mean that the defense is so good at either stopping the run or stopping the pass, that they give opponents no chance to use that strategic option.

I encourage you to teach your defense to be so effective against the run that the other team is forced to pass, or so effective against the pass that the other team is forced to run. Once you eliminate half of the offense's options, you can shut it down.

Emphasize Team

Offensive coaches are always trying to create one-on-one or isolation situations. But you don't want to encourage individual play on the defensive side. The best defense is a team defense—players working together on every play to stop the offense.

For example, a good defensive lineman might have to occupy two offensive linemen to keep the blockers off the linebackers. Or, a linebacker or defensive end might have to block or hold up an offensive receiver to help a deep back in pass coverage.

For this reason we never emphasize who is the leading tackler, who gets the most sacks, or who gets the most interceptions. The individual stats simply reflect how well the guys next to you did their jobs. And some player stats, like middle linebackers' leading a team in tackles, are more a function of positioning than of individual achievement.

Keep it Basic

Whether you use a defensive scheme geared toward stopping the run or stopping the pass, keep it simple. Although you may understand and feel you can teach complex defensive strategies, consider whether the costs of players' poor learning, confusion, indecision, and frustration are worth it.

The most effective defensive schemes are the most basic. The scheme will work if it can adjust to handle a variety of offenses and situations and if it can effectively shut down the run or the pass.

The defensive system you select might be simple, but encourage your defensive players to play smart. If an offense goes into a no-huddle on a drive, your defense should be able to respond, even if the offense throws some new wrinkles at it.

The "smarts" with which your defense plays directly reflects its preparation. Make your defense meet all kinds of situations in practice that it might face in a game. See if the defense can respond to different offensive looks by learning the principles of your defensive scheme. In short, test your team

defense on the practice field before your players get to the battle field.

Defensive Styles

Do you want to have a pressure defense, or do you prefer the bend-but-don't-break approach? These are fundamental questions every coach must answer. And when considering what style of defense to adopt, always factor in how it would work with your team's offensive style.

Some defensive-minded coaches don't think about their offense when they implement their defensive scheme. For example, they might combine a bend-but-don't-break defense with a 3-yards-and-a-cloud-of-dust offense. But the two are like oil and water.

The reason is that the ground-it-out offense needs the ball consistently near midfield to score. It will rarely go 70 yards on a drive. Yet the bend-but-don't-break defense will often give you poor field position and so it must be matched with an offense capable of moving the length of the field. That's why you need a pressure-type, aggressive defense to complement a conservative running game. Conversely, if you have a potent offense that gains yardage in big chunks, you can afford the bend-but-don't-break style.

Choosing a Defensive Alignment

As I explained in chapter 11, defensive formations are indentified by how many players are on the line of scrimmage and where they line up relative to the offensive center. Even defenses have no noseguard directly across from the center; odd defenses do.

In determining how many players to put on the line of scrimmage, first consider the scheme and style of defense you want. Do you prefer to attack the offense or to sit and read the offense?

Other big factors to consider are your personnel and the schedule you play. Do you have several quality linemen? Is the strength of your team its quickness or its size? Do you have an aggressive noseguard for the 5-2? Do you have a strong middle linebacker for a 4-3?

And what about your opponents? Do most emphasize the run or do they emphasize the pass? How do they match up physically? What are their common offensive formations?

Think through all of these questions far before your first practice. Then select the defensive alignment most advantageous to your personnel and system and least advantageous to your opponents' strengths.

The 7-Man Front vs. the 8-Man Front

Now let's look at two types of defensive alignments and examine their strengths and weaknesses. Almost all defensive formations, at all levels of play, can be lumped into one of two categories: 7-man fronts or 8-man fronts.

7-Man Front

Most pro and college teams put some combination of seven linemen and linebackers on the line of scrimmage. Because the 7-man front has four defensive backs, it adjusts easily to different offensive formations, especially passing, one-back formations. Two common 7-man fronts are the 5-2 and the 4-3 (see Figure 13.1, a and b).

The 7-man front also can be effective against run formations. If you have an aggressive cornerback who can rotate up on running plays, you have the equivalent of an 8-man front.

8-Man Front

This alignment works well against opponents who emphasize the run. By placing so many men on the line, you make it more difficult for the offense to block everyone at the point of attack.

Two common formations used in 8-man front defenses are the 5-3 and the 4-4 (see Figure 13.2, a and b). This defensive alignment matches well against run-oriented offensive formations such as the wishbone and Wing-T. The extra man up front makes it that much tougher for the offense to spring a back through the defensive wall.

The 8-man front is less effective against passing teams and especially against offenses that spread the field to throw. For

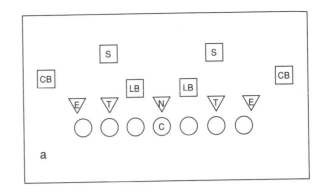

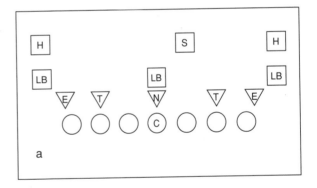

Figure 13.1   Two common 7-man defensive fronts: (a) the 5-2 and (b) the 4-3.

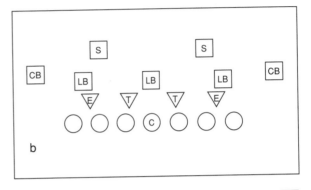

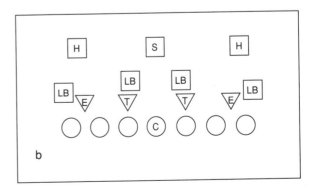

Figure 13.2   Two common formations used in 8-man front defenses: (a) the 5-3 and (b) the 4-4.

instance, trying to cover a slot man with a linebacker or end poses a real mismatch. It also is harder to adjust to multiple spread formations with only three defensive backs.

Augustana 5-2 Rover Defense

The 5-2 rover formation (see Figure 13.3) allows our team to adjust easily to changing offensive formations against both the run and the pass. We also believe this defense is effective as our pressure defense and that it emphasizes our defensive players' strengths.

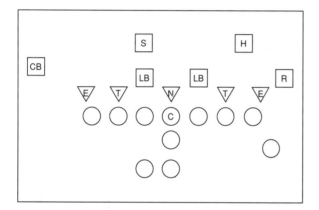

Figure 13.3   The 5-2 rover defense.

This defense places our rover in the teeth of the offense, no matter what formation we face (see Figures 13.4 and 13.5). That is why our rover is one of our best and toughest players. If the offense is going to beat us, it's

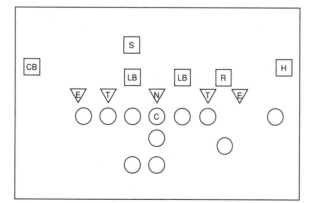

Figure 13.4   The 5-2 rover against a Wing-T.

going to beat our best. What often happens is the opposing offense becomes so concerned with avoiding our rover, that it abandons what it does best.

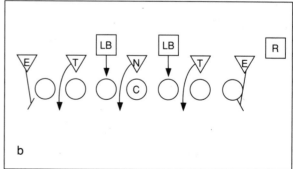

Figure 13.5   The 5-2 rover against a pro set.

Line and Linebacker Options

The real test of our 5-2 rover defensive formation comes when the ball is snapped. Within our pressure defense concept, the 5-2 front can slant, blitz, or cross.

The 5-slant and 3-slant (see Figure 13.6,

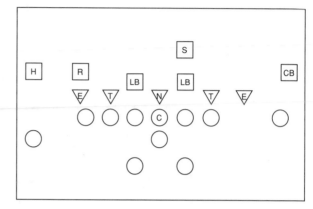

a

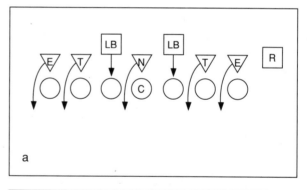

b

Figure 13.6   The 5-2 rover defense executes (a) a 5-slant and (b) a 3-slant.

a and b) create one defensive alignment, which, when you slant the line, transforms into a different defense.

We also can blitz out of the 5-2 (see Figure 13.7) to confuse and pressure the offense. The running start by the linebacker and the slight delay allow the linebacker to seek a seam in the offensive line to attack.

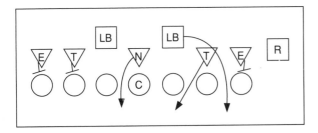

Figure 13.7 The 5-2 rover defense executes a blitz.

And sometimes we cross (see Figure 13.8) our linebacker and noseguard to penetrate the middle.

Of course, if the blitz is countered you have overcommitted your defense and the offense might discover a big play.

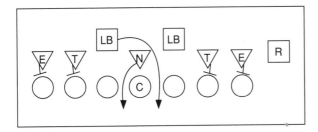

Figure 13.8 The 5-2 rover defense executes a cross.

Down and Distance Strategies

Three factors help us decide when to use which tactic. First: our defensive scheme. Second: what down it is. Third: how far the offense has to go for a first down. As I've said, we prefer to pressure the opponent defensively because our offense is a ball-control system. It doesn't make sense for us to sit back and read on defense and then hope our offense can drive the length of the field.

  FIELD POSITION A PRIORITY

When I came to Augustana, we had an outstanding defensive coordinator, Mike Hollway, now head football coach at Ohio Wesleyan University. Because Mike was such a capable coach, about the only comment I ever made to him that first year was to set the goal line on field position. By that I meant we could not allow the other team to drive the length of the field and then try to stop it at the goal line.

In other words, I didn't think our offense could drive 70 or 80 yards very often. So I was telling Mike that if we were able to make three first downs, our defense could give up only two first downs.

We had to pressure all over the field and be patient on offense for a chance to score. We did that, and in the process established a style of defensive play at Augustana. In the very first year we achieved a 6-3 record from what had been a losing program.

Offenses develop down-and-distance tendencies, calling the same or similar plays on certain downs with a specified number of yards to go. For instance, they call fullback screens and draw plays on 2nd down and 10-20 yards for a 1st down. The more you know about the opponent, the more you can predict its offense in certain situations.

Using a computer, today's major college and professional teams zero in on a team's tendencies and call defenses accordingly.

Let's say your scouting reports indicate that on 3rd-and-short yardage the opponent likes to sweep to the wide side of the field. The defensive call could be a total line slant toward the wide side to force the play.

Team Defensive Drills

Pursuit Drill

Purpose. To teach the defense proper pursuit angles that prevent a big offensive play

Procedure. The defense lines up in regular alignment. The quarterback takes the snap and throws a quick pass to one of the two receivers on the sideline. After the catch, the receiver runs toward the goal line with the entire defense *sprinting* in pursuit (see Figure 13.9). Repeat the drill with stunts called before the snap to insure proper lanes.

Coaching Points. Be sure the defense runs the proper angle to be able to catch the

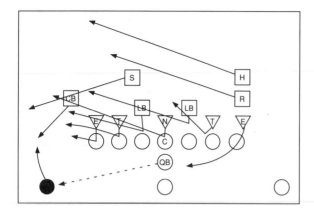

Figure 13.9 The entire defense is in pursuit after the receiver.

ballcarrier. Also be sure defenders don't follow one another. They should pursue at different angles.

Adjustment Drill

Purpose. To have the whole defensive team recognize and adjust to offensive formations and shifts

Procedure. The defense lines up in its regular alignment. The offense goes into formation, then shifts or sends a man in motion. The defense must recognize, adjust, and react to the play run by the offense (see Figure 13.10, a and b). The offense should present a variety of formations and shifts for the defense to read and respond to.

Coaching Points. This drill helps your team learn to apply your defensive principles. Make sure to require adjustment from all parts of your defense rather than isolate one area.

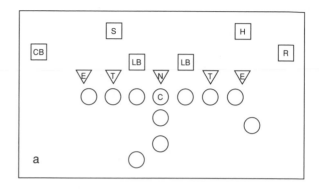

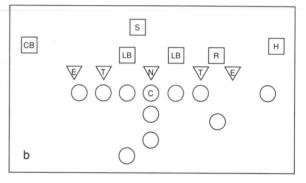

Figure 13.10 (a) Basic defense vs. Wing-T and (b) switch of rover and corner to Wing-T with split end.

Recognition and Reaction Drill

Purpose. To teach the defense to recognize the formation, adjust to it, and to think about the offensive team's tendencies

Procedure. Offensive teams break huddle, line up, and run a play. The defense reacts accordingly, "wrapping up" the ballcarrier.

Coaching Points. Check for proper alignment, pursuit, and recognition of tendencies.

Summary

1. Defense is a team game. The line, the linebacker, and the defensive backs must be coordinated.
2. Primary considerations for choosing a defensive scheme are your personality, your personnel, and your schedule.
3. Your defense should complement your offense.
4. Once you choose a defense, learn how to make it work most effectively against each offense you face.
5. Key on offensive down and distance tendencies, and don't take unnecessary gambles on defense.

Chapter 14

Teaching the Kicking Game

Any veteran coach or knowledgeable fan knows something important is missing from the techniques and tactics we've covered so far in Parts III and IV. In this chapter we'll look at the kicking game, also called special teams play. But don't infer that this position in the book reflects the importance I place on the kicking game. I respect it as often the difference between winning and losing.

The late George Allen was one of the first and foremost coaches to emphasize special teams. He made his players believe it was an honor to be one of the 11 guys selected to a kick unit. After Allen's Rams and Redskins won so many games on their special teams performances, other coaches began to take the kicking game more seriously. Now every pro and college team has a special teams coach, and every smart coach makes the kicking game a priority, not an afterthought.

In a chapter, I can't teach the kicking game in the depth it deserves because each play has skill positions that require correct and repeated techniques. To cover them all in detail would take an entire book.

But in this chapter we will address the primary components of each special team situation—kickoffs, field goals, and punts.

Start with this information when you teach your players, then get more specific with players at each skill position.

Kickoff

The kickoff is a fun part of football. It allows coaches to use high-spirited, aggressive players who like to get after the other team. For years, Texas A&M has had a kickoff team composed of walk-ons from the student body. These effective and enthusiastic players allow starters to rest and reduce the injury rate among starters, who otherwise would be on the kick team.

A throw-caution-to-the-wind attitude can be helpful, but even kickoff team members need discipline. Each player will have certain responsibilities, perhaps breaking up the return team's "wedge," filling lanes of pursuit, or holding back as contain men.

The kickoff team begins, but does not end, with the kicker. Sometimes, one strong-legged player stands out among the others. Other times, the kicker emerges from competition with teammates. Kicking is objective, and the person who kicks the highest and farthest is your kickoff man.

The other players on the kickoff team should be fast, strong, and sure tacklers.

You'll want at least one especially fast player on each end of the kick formation to sprint down the field after the return man. You'll also want heftier, linebacker types in the middle of the formation to bust up any wedge the return team may try to form. Finally, the kicker or a contain man on each side should hang back to prevent a TD return (see Figure 14.1).

Because the kickoff squad is often the first to represent your team in a game, its performance can set the tone for other phases of the game. The field position your kickoff team gives the opponent's offense also can have important consequences for your defense.

Besides using your strongest kicker, practice the skill of kicking away from your opponent's best return man. At times, a no-return, flat kick is used to disrupt the timing of a great return team.

Kickoff Return

If your team ever leads the nation in kickoff returns, you had a bad season. It means your opponents kicked off a lot because they scored on you a lot.

But on a more positive note, a great kickoff return can establish excellent field position for your offense at the start of a half, or it can change the game's momentum after an

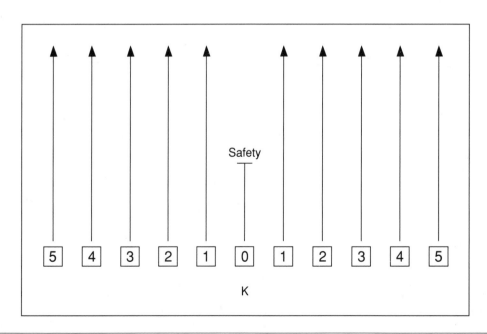

Figure 14.1   The kickoff team's position.

opponent scores. When executed well, the return can be football's most exciting play.

On a return, you'll typically station your two or three fastest and most elusive open-field runners at the deep positions. Ahead of them will be good blocking from mobile players such as tight ends and fullbacks. Up front you'll want bigger, agile linemen who have good hands, in case the kick team tries to kick short.

The simplest and most used kick return is based on the math principle that the shortest distance between two points is a straight line. In this return, the front five or six and the middle group of returners form a wedge between the returner and the opponent's goal (see Figure 14.2). This allows the returner to get a full running start and to look for any hole in the kick coverage. The kicking team tries to run around or fight through the wedge of blockers.

Field Goal and Point After Touchdown

The field goal and extra point were once described by the late Dave Nelson, secretary of the NCAA football rules committee, as the "unstoppable play." But when rule changes did away with the tee and narrowed the goal-

posts, the can't-miss play suddenly became much less a sure thing.

Whether it's 3 points or 1 point, take these scoring opportunities seriously. Work with your skill people to make field goals and points after touchdowns (PAT) as automatic as possible. What may seem like wasted practice time can mean the winning margin in two or three games a season.

A basic field goal or PAT alignment is shown in Figure 14.3. (The holder would be on the left side of a left-footed kicker.)

This is a tight formation whose basic rule is that each blocker is responsible for his inside gap. The blockers must provide the kicker a pocket in which to kick the ball.

Every position on a field goal/PAT team is important, but some roles are especially vital. Here are the three most important roles on the field goal and PAT units and ways to teach those players to fulfill their duties.

Center

First, you need a center who can snap the ball deep, about 7 yards. This is a special skill requiring much practice.

The center must spread his legs wider apart for the deep snap because he has to throw his arms backward between his legs. The center must place both hands on the ball: The under hand is the power hand; the

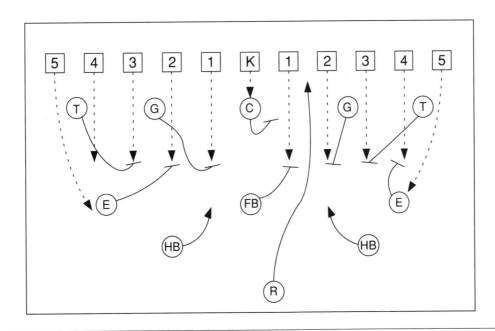

Figure 14.2 A kickoff return.

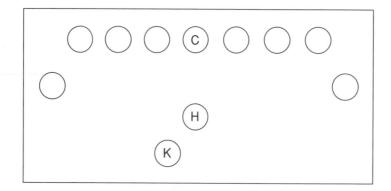

Figure 14.3   A basic field goal or PAT alignment.

top hand is the guide hand that puts the ball into a tight spiral. The center should focus on the holder's hands, specifically the hand nearest the spot of the hold.

This is such an important task that the center is not expected to block on the kick. Any center who can block, of course, is a plus.

In college you can recruit centers who can snap. In high school you often have to use whomever can get the job done best.

Holder

The holder is the quarterback of the extra-point team. He is responsible for the lineup, the signal count, and placing the ball for the kicker.

The holder kneels 7 yards behind the center and marks a spot where the kicker knows he will set the ball. The holder should try to catch the ball at arm's length (arms toward the center) and then quickly move the ball to the spot. As he sets the tip of the ball on the ground, the holder may have to turn the ball so the kicker doesn't kick it on the laces.

The holder must have sure and quick hands. He must spot the ball for the kicker in proper position within 2.5 seconds after the snap. Any slower, and the kicker's timing will be ruined and the kick probably will be blocked.

Field-Goal Kicker

Field-goal kicking is perhaps the most specialized skill in football. Perhaps that is why players who seem unlikely football athletes are successful at it; they have focused entire practice sessions on one skill—kicking the ball through the uprights.

Make no mistake, field-goal kicking doesn't happen by chance. It must be practiced extensively and regularly.

Here are things to watch for to help your kicker with his field-goal technique:

1. Keeps his head down, focuses on the spot of the ball.
2. Plants the nonkicking foot alongside the football, not behind or in front.
3. Extends the leg on follow-through.

 COACH CAN'T TAKE CREDIT

In 1986 we had three outstanding high school kickers in our area. One was a punt-pass-and-kick champion who later kicked for the University of Iowa. Another became a 4-year, first-string kicker at Northern Illinois University. The third was my oldest son, Barry, who became a 1990 Kodak All-American at Augustana.

A local newspaper interviewed all three players when they were in high school. The reporter assumed I had taught Barry how to kick. Barry corrected the reporter, telling him he picked up kicking on his own while attending countless football practices as a child. When bored, he'd go to one end of the field and kick the football. He truly was a self-taught kicker, learning the skill from repeated practice—not from his dad's instruction.

Faking the Field Goal or PAT

It is best to fake a field goal or PAT when your opponent least expects it. Practicing a fake from that formation probably will help you control the rush-block attempt and also will train your team to organize when a bad center snap or some other mistake occurs.

Punting

We never like it, but even the most potent offensive team will have to punt on occasion. Look at punting as a way to get out of trouble or as a way to give your team better field position.

Center

On punts, the center will have to snap the ball about 13 yards. The technique is much as for the field-goal snap. But because the distance and height of the snap are greater,

the center will need even more power from his under hand.

The center should zero in on the punter's belt buckle from the beginning of the snap count until the ball reaches the punter's hands. His blocking responsibility is not nearly as important as his role of getting a fast, accurate snap to the punter.

 NO SCRAMBLING AT THIS POSITION

In 1976, our back-up deep snapper for the state championship game was our quarterback. As luck would have it, our first-string snapper suffered an injury, so the quarterback had to snap the ball on punts, field goals, and extra points. He performed his role flawlessly. But you better believe the opposing defensive linemen showed him no mercy after he got rid of the ball. It was their way of welcoming the quarterback to the trenches.

Punter

The punt, or free kick, requires a very different kicking motion than does the placekick used in kickoffs, field goals, and PATs. And yet much of the same discipline and repetition required to be a good placekicker is also required to become a good punter.

Here are four important points you should teach your punter:

1. Watch the snap. Be sure to catch the ball, then kick it.
2. Never take more than two steps before punting. Your first step must be with your kicking foot.
3. Step straight in the direction you are kicking.
4. Line the ball up and set it (slightly drop it) on your foot with toe extended.

One of the best ways punters can practice fundamentals is to have them kick short punts, like a quarterback throws short passes. This develops the punter's concentration on placing the ball on his extended foot and on getting the ball to spiral like a pass.

Besides teaching correct form, work with your punters on punting strategy. Set up rewards for kicking the ball out of bounds inside the opponent's 15-yard line rather than into the end zone.

Also have the punter and the punting team take real pride in the *net* yards of punts, not the length of the kicks. It does no good to kick the ball 50 yards if the opponent's going to return it 25 yards. I'd rather have a 35-yard punt with no return.

Punt Formations

Here are two basic types of punt formations. In the tight formation (see Figure 14.4), the punter takes the snap 10 yards behind the center. You'd use this formation to compensate for a poor center or to kick the ball from your own end zone.

The more common punt formation is the spread alignment shown in Figure 14.5. In this case the punter lines up 13 to 15 yards behind the center.

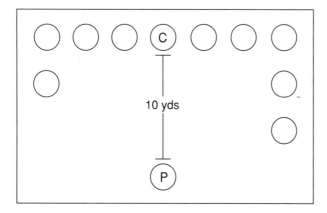

Figure 14.4 The tight punt formation.

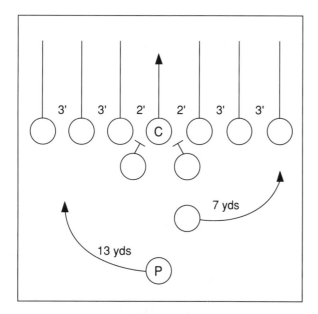

Figure 14.5 The spread punt formation.

Punt Coverage

The key to a successful punt team is not necessarily how far the punter can kick the ball but how well the rest of the team gets downfield and tackles the returner. It is better to kick 40 yards and allow a 5-yard return than to kick 50 yards and allow a 20-yard return.

Punt coverage is the ability to contain the return. A spread formation helps the coverage in that the kicker is back 13 to 15 yards, which allows the line to block for a shorter time and cover a longer distance.

Formation, however, cannot make up for attitude. All good punt teams need aggressive, fast players who sprint hard to the ball. Proper spacing is necessary to prevent holes from opening up for the return. Your punter usually will be the safety, holding back in case the runner breaks free.

Punt Return

The punt return is a big play. A good return puts the offense in good field position and sets a positive tone for the beginning of a drive.

The return begins with good pressure on the kicker. When you spot a hole in the punting team's formation or have a team pinned back in its territory, you may want to try to block the kick. Your punt return team should be disciplined enough to go after the block while avoiding a roughing-the-kicker call, which can give the ball back to the punting team's offense.

After the rush, the next component of the punt return—blocking for the punt returner—takes precedence. Players must block above the waist and make sure that the head is in front of an opponent before they make contact. Many excellent punt returns have been called back because of a clipping penalty.

You may choose to use one, two, or even three deep men to return the punt. The advantage of one man back and a 10-man rush is a slower coverage by the punting team. However, a good kicker will kick away from the one returner and get the punt to roll. The average roll of a punt is about 10 yards—more on artificial surfaces.

The punt returner must catch well and remain aware of his posiiton on the field. For instance, he needs to take advantage of the fair catch when the punt team's coverage is on top of him, but to let the ball go into the end zone for a touchback when it's apparent it will do so.

Wall Return

A common punt return play is to set up a wall of blockers to spring the runner free down a sideline. As you can see in Figure 14.6, the wall return involves flooding one side of the field with blockers to form a barrier against the punting team's tacklers.

The play begins with the end on the side of the return pushing his man out. The tackle next to him pushes his man in. This small adjustment will create an alley for the returns farther downfield. The end and tackle then sprint downfield to form the front of the wall. The linebacker hits the guard and follows the tackle to the wall. The noseguard hits the snapper and follows the linebacker to the wall.

The tackle and end on the side of the field away from the return rush the punter and try to force him to kick quickly. The backside linebacker blocks the first opponent down. The backs seal inside and lead the return man. Note from the diagram that the back on the return side blocks in to let the return man get started. The other back protects the returner, then leads to block the contain man. The return man will threaten the middle, then break to the wall following his lead back. The return man's job is to make it to the other side of the wall that his teammates have built for him.

 PUNT RETURN PROWESS

In the late 1960s, during our record-setting winning streak in high school, we had a safety return 15 punts for TDs of over 60 yards in his last 14 games. The player was Barry Pearson, later a member of the Steelers and the Chiefs. His ability inspired the whole team to give extra effort.

Special Teams Practice

Special teams practice is just that. I believe that you must practice all phases of the kicking game live and at full speed.

We practice punting live every day but work on live kickoffs and kickoff returns less

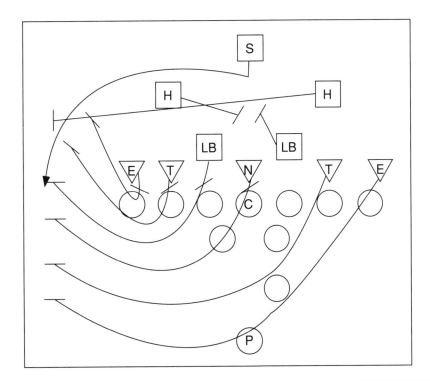

Figure 14.6 In the wall return, blockers flood one side of the field to form a barrier against the punting team's tacklers.

often because of the injury possibilities from open-field blocks and tackles.

Our drills consist of individuals practicing their skills on their own—punts, extra points, or kickoffs. When we drill as a team, it is our full-speed, full-contact kicking team.

Summary

1. The kicking game is a third of a football game. Give it at least a third of your attention.
2. Help players develop specialized skills to excel at the kicking game. Kicking camps, books, videos, and extra individual instruction can be very important to their development.
3. Special teams are, well, special. Treat them as such with attention at practice and responsibilities in games.

Part V

Coaching Games

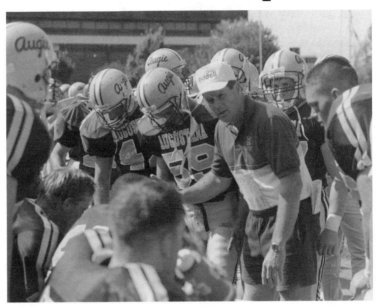

Chapter 15

Preparing for Games

Preparing for games starts with preparing to practice. By that I mean if we have readied our players physically and emotionally during the week, we should be set to perform on game day.

Everything you do before the first game and between games should benefit the players' readiness for taking the field against the next opponent. Each scouting report, drill, and meeting should give your team a better chance of succeeding in the upcoming contest. This preparation process should become a routine, efficient pattern.

Focusing on the Game

Preparation for the next game begins when one game ends. Emotions associated with the previous game may stick with you a day or two, but your thoughts should shift to the next game, the next opponent. We've found that this shift in focus from the just-completed game to the next contest helps us avoid getting too low or too high.

One important part of preparation is the rest and healing players must have after a game. We encourage players to get immediate attention from the trainer for anything bothering them. And we tell them to get good nourishment and sleep well during the 24 hours after the game so their bodies recover. Failure to see the trainer or get proper rest can hamper them at the next week's practices.

When we gather Monday for practice, we expect everyone to be ready to go. We'll follow the same practice schedule for each game (chapter 6). This routine builds or maintains our players' physical conditioning and gets them mentally prepared and peaked for the game.

 NOT JUST ANY NUMBER

One coach I know tried a special approach to get his team psyched up for an opening game. The first day of practice, his players noticed a huge number posted on the locker-room wall. No one knew what it meant. Each day the number got smaller. Finally, the last week before the game, the players realized that it was the number of minutes until the first kickoff. The players began counting down the minutes too, totally focused on the start of the game.

Focusing on the Opposition

A lot of coaches excuse a poor performance by saying their players were "looking ahead" to a strong upcoming opponent. I don't buy that excuse. Sure, players know who is going to be good on the schedule, but the coaches must make sure players go into every game with the same degree of mental preparation.

We have never felt our teams had a problem with looking past an opponent. We remind players each day that it is their individual responsibility to use the work days to get ready for game day.

 OPPONENT IN REFLECTION

I used to put the name of our opponent on the mirror. When the players combed their hair,

they couldn't avoid thinking about that opponent. It was right in front of them.

After the game, if we were successful, we placed the name of the opposition on the left side of the mirror; if we failed, it went on the right side of the mirror. We were hoping that at the end of the season the right side would be bare.

It became traditional to place the next opponent's name on the the locker-room mirror. After a while the kids began doing it themselves at the beginning of each week. I believe it helped our players stay focused on who we were playing each week.

Coaches must study the opponent and teach players what they need to know to have the best chance of being successful. It begins with scouting and ends with the final practice before the game.

Scouting

Scouting is paramount because football is such a patterned game. Where you position your players versus the opponent is crucial. Football is not a simple game of reaction; players need to be positioned properly and to have rehearsed ways to counteract what the opposition does.

Our week of formal preparation begins with the coaching staff receiving the scouting report. We receive this information the day after the game, and immediately begin to break it down.

Teams scout in several ways. Some use film. Others use audiocassette play-by-play

descriptions. Many use written reports. Most programs, in fact, use a combination of the three scouting methods.

Conferences typically have rules governing film exchange between schools. These guidelines establish the content and quality of the film, plus the time frame for sending it to the next opponent. But when you get into the playoffs against nonconference schools, sometimes schools ignore the common film exchange courtesies.

 THE WRONG FILM

To prepare for a 1983 playoff game, we began analyzing a game film sent to us by our next opponent. It didn't take long to see something was wrong.

The team was known for having a very good quarterback. Yet the film the school sent us showed only the second-team quarterback in action.

We didn't want to play without seeing the opponent's most potent offensive weapon, so we called that school and requested another film. They acted surprised but agreed (at the insistance of the NCAA) to send us another game film—one showing their first-team quarterback.

Film Analysis

Assuming we have the proper film exchange, we immediately break it down. If you can afford sophisticated technology, you can program a computer to sort plays in every possible manner.

We first break down the film into the opponent's offense, defense, and special teams. Within these categories, we then look at specific elements within each unit.

Film analysis should expose that team's tendencies you can use to your advantage. A careful examination will detect subtle changes in alignment or personnel that will give the play away. For example, you'll find some teams have definite run formations and use different formations for pass plays.

Advantages of Film

If used wisely, film is great: It gives you a chance to watch an opponent you'd otherwise be unable to see because of conflicting game schedules. Without film, our scouting would be based solely on the written and oral reports from our scouts.

Film is a great teacher and helps with good game planning. Although you can never be

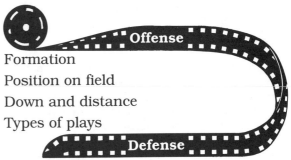

Offense
Formation
Position on field
Down and distance
Types of plays

Defense
Base defense
Defensive adjustments to different offensive sets
Individual responsibilities

Special Teams
Alignments
Blocking schemes
Best coverage men

100% sure what an opponent might do, film lets you plan for the next game with some degree of certainty and helps you build confidence in yourself, your coaching staff, and your players.

Disadvantages of Film

Although film as a scouting tool has many advantages, it also has limitations. Film does not capture the physical capabilities of an opponent, nor give you a feel for game conditions. Film rarely allows you to see the actions of all 11 of their players on the field. And because the camera usually stops between plays, you don't see how the team substitutes or learn much about the attitudes of individual players.

Film also can be costly. And even with computer technology to break down content, film requires extensive time to program and gather data into meaningful parts.

Another caution: Make sure your players don't get overconfident or discouraged after watching the opponent. Emphasize that players should study the opponent's technique and patterns. Don't let players form opinions based on how successful your next opponent was (in the game on film).

 THE WRONG PICTURE

In my first year at a high school, I used a film from the previous year to help prepare for an

opponent. In that film, the team ran its offense out of a Wing-T, so I geared a defensive alignment and scheme to stop plays from that formation.

You can imagine my surprise when the opponent's sophomore team's offense ran from a double-wing with an offset fullback. Our coaching staff went to the locker room immediately to devise a last-minute defensive adjustment that would be effective if the varsity also ran from that formation. It didn't help. Our defensive players were out of position all night because we had failed to prepare them correctly in our practices.

After the game, we found the film we had studied for the game had been placed in the wrong container. The team we had scouted on film was not the same school we had just played.

That incident highlights the need for accurate recordkeeping, for proper storage of all game films, and, of course, for good scouts.

Scouting Report

Because film is not a perfect way to study an opponent, the old-fashioned form of scouting is still popular. One or two people you trust attend the opponent's game or games preceding your contest. They record on paper, audiocassette, or both information you have asked for.

Typically included in that information are the team's basic alignments, its favorite offensive plays, and its key players. This can be recorded on a scouting form. Our scouting report lets you keep track of the down, distance, and field position. For easy tabulation, always write the position of the down in the same place on the scouting form (e.g., 1st down always in the upper left, 2nd down upper right, 3rd down lower left, and 4th down lower right).

You'll also want the scouts to provide special insights. For instance, does an opposing player tip off plays? Perhaps an offensive guard lines up farther back when he is going to pull on a sweep or trap. If so, you can alert your defense to key on the guard and anticipate the play. Your scouts should always look for ways you can gain an edge.

Scouts also must find the other team's strengths. For example, if the team has a fast and elusive split end, you may need to put two defensive backs on him. You can't ask a player to do what he is physically incapable of doing.

Two scouts are better than one. With two you can get both written and tape-recorded accounts of the opponent. If the scouts are responsible, you will get a high degree of consistency between the two reports, which increases your confidence in the information you've received.

 SCOUTING THE WRONG SQUAD

My first year at Geneseo, a coach was sent out to scout a great team that had lost only one game that year. That team was fast: The backfield consisted of all four members of the state championship 440-relay team. The coach returned with a one-page scouting report. A note in its right corner said, "Check out the third cheerleader from the left; she's really neat." Talk about being upset. I said, "No wonder you people never win anything around here." Because it was the final game, that coach finished the season, but it was his last at our school.

Self-Scouting

If I have given the impression that our biggest concern in preparing for a game is what the opponent does, I have misled you. We are always much more concerned with our own team's performance than we are with the opponent.

That's true of most coaches I know. In fact, I suspect that most of the film coaches watch is to scout their own team, not the opponent.

Although we probably do know our team best, sometimes that familiarity causes oversights. Because we are so close to the situation, we may miss tendencies we've developed. Perhaps we have established a pattern in play selection on certain downs and distances. Maybe it is something as simple as the quarterback always calling for the snap count. Without an outside or more objective perspective—through film or written reports—you might not catch such habits.

Think of what you are trying to detect in your opponents. Then think of what your opponents might detect when they scout you.

Coach to Self, Not the Opponent

Our emphasis on self-scouting is part of a bigger philosophy that says, "Be more concerned with what you do than with what the opposition does." We can control much more of what we do than what our opponent does.

Even if you make a scrupulous, time-consuming scouting effort on an opponent, you

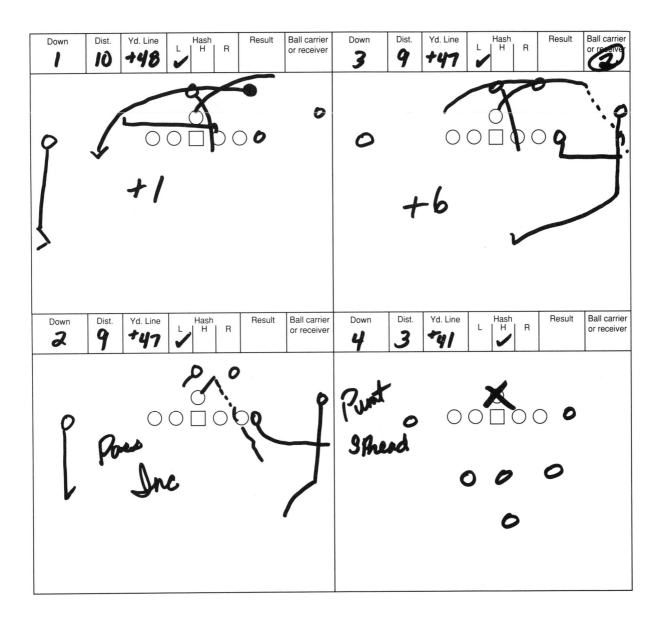

can't hang your hat on it. How a team plays against one opponent is not necessarily how it will play against you. That was apparent during our 52-game undefeated string in high school and later during our 60-game winning string in college. During both streaks, teams threw all kinds of junk offenses and defenses at us in hopes of knocking us off.

We've never tried to hide or camouflage what we do. As Adolph Rupp once said to fellow conference coaches who were attending his basketball camp: "You may know what we do, but until you step out on that court against us, you won't know how well we do it."

Other teams know exactly what Augie will do, yet we know that if we do it well enough,

it doesn't matter. No team will stop us unless it is far superior physically.

Preparing the Game Plan

Scouting reports are worthwhile only if you use them to develop the game plan: the general and specific schemes, tactics, and plays you will emphasize *from your base offense and defense.*

You don't create a game plan from scratch for each contest. Because you have only a week to prepare, your players will have trouble grasping even modest tactical changes. So the game is really a refinement or tailoring of your strategy—your game plan—to accentuate your strengths and expose your opponent's weakness.

LEAVING WELL ENOUGH ALONE

Before one championship, the coaching staff felt so confident about our knowledge of the opponent's offense that we shared a lot of information with our defensive players about how to stop that offense. We even designed a special defense that we felt was sure to work.

Our confidence in the defensive game plan ended as soon as the opponent marched straight downfield after the opening kickoff. We didn't have much more success stopping it the entire first half.

At halftime we switched back to our base defense—the one we had used successfully for 13 games. Freed of our special defensive strategy, the players reacted quicker and more instinctively to the ball. We gave up only 3 points the second half, and claimed a national championship.

The "What Ifs"

In addition to the standard game plan, a coach must consider many "what ifs": What if the opponent goes to a no-huddle offense? What if we can't handle their noseguard one-on-one? What if we are 1 point down, with less than 2 minutes left, and have to choose between kicking an extra point for a tie or going for a 2-point conversion?

The head coach, with input from his assistants, must know the answers to "what ifs." Many coaches plot their responses before game day. Others prefer to decide on the spot, taking into consideration such factors as momentum, injuries, and recommendations from players.

If the "what ifs" aren't complicated enough, factor in all the possible decisions an opposing coach could make. Will he have his punter fake on 4th-and-4 from the 50-yard line? Will he switch from a 7-man defensive front to an 8-man front in an effort to stop the running game?

Obviously, you can't plan for or predict every contingency. Too many inexperienced coaches make futile efforts to do so, and in the process lose sight of what should be their primary concern: preparing their team.

We present our players the fewest possible "what if" scenarios. The fewer options they have to consider, the better. We want our players confident about what they as individuals and as a team are doing. We don't want them concerned about what the opponent might do. That's the coach's privilege.

Implementing the Game Plan

Now that you know what information we acquire and what we emphasize in preparing for games, let's look at how we put that information and philosophy to work. Here is a description of how we prepare our plan for each game.

Monday

The coaching staff meets and determines how, from our base offense and base defense, we can best attack the opponent. We don't want to eliminate any of our options from the plan.

Then we look more closely at our offense, defense, and special teams in light of the opponent's strengths and weaknesses. From this analysis we ask a series of questions:

On offense: What series will we emphasize?
   What plays will work best from that series?
   What specific personnel mismatches can we exploit?

On defense: How will we cover various formations?
   What plays or individuals must we stop first?
   How does our personnel match up?

On special teams: How do they line up?
   What are their strengths?

Part of our evaluation will include the opponent's tendencies: what they run in certain down-and-distance situations; how we might take advantage of these tendencies; what keys to look for in their defense; how we can help our quarterback and receivers identify these keys. This evaluation and planning often take us into the next day when we must be ready to communicate the game plan to our players.

Tuesday

The team's first taste of the game plan comes at this afternoon's practice. Actually, we introduce a specific game plan to each unit—offense, defense, and all of the special teams.

The method of instruction is an on-the-field chalk talk. This approach lets players better grasp the formations and plays by moving through them rather than just viewing them on a chalkboard. At this time we show them adjustments we will make to our base offense and defense and any new wrinkle to the kicking game.

After walking through the game plan as whole units, players break into small groups and work on individual techniques and group tactics that are most important for that week. For instance, if we are playing a team that throws often to its running backs, our linebackers will complete pass defense drills to work on their coverage techniques.

When this small-group drill work is completed, we will again gather the offensive and defensive units (at opposite ends of the field). Each unit tries to execute the game plan and employ techniques they were taught earlier in the practice. A scout team impersonates the opponent and mimics as best it can the next opponent's formations, plays, and tendencies.

Wednesday

It's nice to imagine that everything we planned on Monday and Tuesday would work just as we predicted, but that is rarely the case. So on Wednesday the coaches meet and evaluate how to revise the game plan. For instance, perhaps we find we cannot use a certain blocking scheme as we thought we would.

If such adjustments are necessary, we introduce them in the same walk-through chalk talk. We want to ensure players understand the change. Then we test whether the changes work in our live scrimmage against the scout team.

On Wednesday we work on executing our kicking game and practice at full speed any adjustments to the opponent's special teams that we introduced on Tuesday.

Wednesday is our true work day, but we feel it also is game day in terms of game preparation. The tempo of Friday's or Saturday's game usually reflects how well we practiced on Tuesday and Wednesday.

Pregame Practice

The day before the game, practice is brief and light, just enough for players to break

a sweat. At this point we should not significantly change the game plan.

We remind players of all of their assignments and have them walk through each part of our offensive, defensive, and special teams plan.

Summary

No football coach or team can walk onto the field and be consistently successful without proper physical and mental preparation. The components of that preparation should include:

1. A familiar and focused practice routine
2. Scouting information obtained through film analysis and written and oral reports
3. An emphasis on self-improvement and better team performance, not on what the opponent does
4. A well-conceived game plan that does not stray far from the base offensive and defensive schemes
5. Careful implementation of the game plan through teaching and practice of tactical components and individual techniques.

Chapter 16

Handling Game Situations

I always believe we can win every game, and I expect my players to believe it too.

It's not overconfidence. We respect everybody on our schedule. And like every coach, I have my share of "what if" thoughts the morning before a game.

But because we believe in our system and in our methods of teaching and preparing, we are confident when we take the field. A big part of this confidence comes from the success we've had over the years. The players have seen what the previous teams accomplished—in other words, tradition.

Pregame

Coaches, like players, must prepare mentally before the game. You can't wait until an hour before kickoff.

In addition to the game plan, you should take into acount a whole set of factors including the game site, the weather, and the motivational level of your players.

Home-Field Advantage?

The home-field advantage in football really isn't as much of a factor as it is in basketball. The size of the field and the distance of the fans from the sidelines limit the home team advantage. And unless you are in a 50,000-seat stadium full of screaming fans, the environment on the road shouldn't be a problem for your team.

The officiating can be more one-sided on the road, but few games are determined alone by officials' calls. So don't set up your players by telling them the officials will be against them on the road.

Some coaches try to put pressure on officials during games. Although I'm sure it sometimes works, most officials resent this kind of badgering and it backfires against the coach and his team.

Most coaches feel more pressure to win at home. You have more of your fans watching you, more is expected of you, and your record at home is one of the first things an administration looks at in whether to keep you as the coach.

 HOME OR AWAY?

My first year at Augustana, we lost our first four home games. (Somehow we won all of our road games.) It didn't take me long to learn that Augustana was never supposed to lose games on its turf. The players even seemed to feel the pressure. So, to relieve the tension before the last home game of the year, I joked with a local civic club, "I think I'll load the guys on a bus and drive them around the block this week. Maybe then we'll finally win a home game."

After the speech a sportscaster said to me, "Bob, that's a great idea. Do it and I'll shoot the film of it."

I said, "Oh, come on, I was just joking. I don't do that kind of junk."

After giving it more consideration (and after casually meeting Dr. Treadway, our college president, who, though pleased with the program, mentioned our not winning at home), I realized the players were hearing from everyone that they couldn't win at home. Maybe they were starting to believe it.

So, I told the players to meet the morning of the game for breakfast together. When I had them all in the locker room that morning, I had the athletic director, John Farwell, bring a big green bus that we had permission to use. At the end of the meeting, I told the players, "Okay, guys, let's go load up the bus and take our trip. We'll stop for breakfast on the way."

They looked at me like I was joking, but soon they caught on and everyone piled into the bus. We drove around a couple of blocks, and by this time everyone was real loose and laughing. It was a great time. If we were going to lose the game, it wasn't going to be because we were tight.

We won the game 12-8, against an opponent bigger and probably more physically gifted. The home losing streak was over.

Everyone has fond memories of that bus trip and of our first win at home. That's the only time I've pulled a stunt like that, but it seemed like the thing to do.

The Weather Factor

You must account for playing conditions. Weather that is windy, rainy, snowy, extremely hot and humid, or bitterly cold will affect the game. You may need to revise the game plan sightly to adjust for conditions. For example, if it is windy and rainy, you might eliminate riskier plays that require passing or a lot of ball handling.

But I want to stress that you should never use weather as an excuse for losing. The weather does not favor anyone. Both teams

have to deal with the same elements. Bad weather makes a game closer, as teams pull in their game plans and score fewer points.

Player Motivation

The best way for me to motivate myself, both when I played and as I coach, is to have some quiet time when I can really think things through. I also encourage our players to find quiet time when they can think about their responsibilities.

When we get on a bus for a road trip, we expect the players to be concentrating on the game because we believe mental practice will prevent mental errors during the game.

It's funny, though, that now half our team has headphones on in the locker room. I wonder if that's the best thing or if it's necessary. Still, I haven't said no to it.

I definitely am not a rah-rah type. I don't give a knock-the-door-down type of speech. That's not my personality, and it shouldn't be necessary. Rarely does it have any lasting, positive effect.

 CREDIBLE MOTIVATION

I don't believe in motivating a boy to try to do something he can't. In other words, I believe it is unfair to coach a boy all week with emotion, saying, "You can block the All-Pro across from you." Then, the first time he gets hit he knows that he hasn't got a chance.

Make players aware of mismatches and develop a scheme that gives them the best chance to succeed and the confidence that they can. Whether you change the blocking scheme, double-team, or whatever, do what you can to help the overmatched player. It is unfair to pump him up and expect him to survive on emotion. He's going to realize you were lying to him the first time he gets hit.

Motivational Aids and Invited Speakers

There's nothing wrong with a coach using a special tape or invited speaker to get players in a better frame of mind. I get great inspiration from such things. And I know a lot of coaches do it.

Many coaches also take the team to a movie the night before a game, a war movie or whatever. I see nothing wrong with that,

but I've never been in a situation where I considered it necessary.

Not Too High or Too Low

The important thing for any coach is to know the squad's temperament. Watch how fast the players get dressed, how enthusiastically they take the field, and whether they are focused on the task at hand during warm-up drills.

Players' attention spans are shorter on game day, so it's not the time to teach them a new tactic or to give them new assignments. Coaches who make big changes just before key games usually are "rewarded" with turnovers, penalties, and missed assignments.

Players are especially susceptible to mental errors during the early phases of a big game. They are so emotionally involved they have difficulty concentrating on what they're supposed to do. Don't add to their distraction by introducing something completely new to them.

Once we take the field for warm-ups, we seldom go back into the locker room until halftime. We like to keep players active and involved in game preparation. If we have done our work during the week, there should be no need to go over the game plan again at that point. Just a few reminders in a pregame end-zone huddle, and we're ready to go.

"Gamers"

Some players definitely don't practice as well as they play in games. In practice they don't make the extra-special play that they make in a game. These "gamers" seem to have a switch that they can turn on only at game time.

But as I've emphasized throughout this book, we don't believe there is such a thing as "not being a practice player." So players who seem to perform better in games than in practice still are not excused from practicing just as hard as their teammates.

Be careful when judging the balance between ability and effort. What may appear to be loafing by a player may not be. It may be that he's so gifted and smooth that he looks like he's dogging it. Yet when we run windsprints, he's always the first or second guy to finish. While the other guys are huffing and puffing, he has barely broken a sweat. Is it fair to criticize him for his natural ability, which makes it appear that he's expending less effort than his teammates?

TRUTH KNOWN BY WOULD-BE TACKLERS

The great former running back, Jim Brown, was sometimes scoffed at by fans and even by coaches for what might have looked like a half-hearted attitude. He took forever to get back to the huddle after he was tackled. He always looked like he was on his last leg—between plays, that is.

But notice that the defenders who tried to bring him down never opened their mouths. They knew firsthand that Brown gave everything he had on each run. While the people in the stands and press box were chastising him for his apparent lack of effort, opposing defensive players were hoping he wouldn't run the ball in their direction.

Pregame and Postgame Prayers

Augustana is a Christian school. We think it is important that our players reflect Christian values such as dignity, respect, and brotherhood; that they see the value in having faith in something more powerful than their own abilities.

A very meaningful way of teaching these principles is through pregame and postgame prayers. Each game we huddle, kneel, and pray as a group before the national anthem and after we have congratulated the opposing team when the game is over.

The pregame prayer usually involves asking for help to do our best—*not* to win. The postgame prayer is more reflective; we express thanks for having had the opportunity to play together and complete the game without injury.

Teaching these values through prayer is much more difficult today, especially at public schools. Parents and community members are telling coaches, "Those are your values, Coach, not ours." So if you coach at a public school, expect resistance to team prayer.

It is amazing that coaches, who share so many beliefs about health, hygiene, fitness, and academics are rebutted for expressing our beliefs about something so fundamentally important as faith. The pregame and postgame prayers are important times for me, and I believe they also are important to players. It is a special situation in which players can express how they think and feel about themselves and each other. I see no reason that should be forbidden.

Game Time

In the huddle before kickoff, players are keyed up and they can't wait to start. Their ability to channel their emotion constructively into the game is the coach's responsibility.

Coach Conduct

Your team will reflect you. If you lose your concentration or composure during the game, your players are likely to do so too.

If you get upset, don't let it linger. You can count on one hand the number of calls that have been changed because a coach challenged an official. So get back into the game—quickly. If you fail to do so, neither you nor your team will get a second chance on game day.

Reactions to Game Events

My reserved coaching style is not an act. That's me. I'm focused on the game and the players. I'm not so emotionally involved in other things. I'm not preoccupied with the officiating.

Similarly, I expect our players to simply go out and play as hard as they can for all 60 minutes. If they are in the game, they need to give 100%. The score of the game or the officials are not their concerns.

My demeanor probably helps our players stay calm during games. For example, speaking to our quarterback during time-outs in the same moderate tone of voice that I do during practice reassures him not to be alarmed. It's a subtle way of saying, "Just go out and execute like you do in practice."

Assistant coaches can handle many of the Xs and Os during the game. I have the responsiblity for players' emotions and behavior.

True Emotion vs. False Emotion

You can't fake it. If you are a highly emotional person, your players will accept your emotion during the game. Players will appreciate seeing that you're in charge and into the game.

Every coach should show some emotion, but it should be genuine and spontaneous, not choreographed for show.

I am most emotional when our young men accomplish what they set out to do. Great individual effort, perhaps an extra-special first-down run, will also spark a positive reaction. But it's not my style to have an emotional response to every play or when a player fulfills his routine assignment.

No Coach Competition

Because football coaches are on opposite sides of the field, the same kind of give-and-take seen by basketball coaches isn't possible. We always try to greet the opposing coaching staff before the game and congratulate them afterward, regardless of the outcome.

Only under exceptional circumstances will I direct comments toward an opposing coach or player. One of those situations is when the coach tries to direct the officials or my team on the field. Then I will step in. He should never chastise our players. Only once have I directed anything more than a sportsmanlike pat on the back to an opposing player.

 CHEAP SHOT COSTLY

It was early in the second half, but the game was already over. We were way out in front and had made plans to substitute for all of our starters on the next offensive series. We always pulled our first-string offense first, because we have no interest in running up the score on anybody.

But then an opposing defender delivered a terrible cheap shot to one of our players. He was hurt. I was very upset. As our trainer checked the player's condition, I remarked to the guilty defender that his behavior would simply force the score to be more embarrassing than it had to be.

We did not substitute as liberally as planned, and we won by a lopsided margin. No cheap shots, just good hard football.

Personnel Adjustments

Football is now a game of specialists with players for every down and situation. A coach who has the numbers and the material to make these personnel changes can benefit.

I've never been big on situational substitutions. If things are going well, why change? So in most cases we are slow to switch personnel during games. The guys who earned the right to start by their work during the week shouldn't be yanked if they make a physical error.

Conversely, I immediately substitute for players who make mental errors. Mental errors are unacceptable. If we take a guy out to get his attention, he may or may not get back into the game. It depends on how well his sub plays. We won't automatically insert the starter again.

Game-Plan Adjustments

We also believe strongly in sticking with our system and game plan until the time and score dictate a change. Tunrnovers and bad breaks should not be reasons for switching schemes in the middle of a contest.

When a team loads up against one part of our offensive series, we simply run another option. Don't be stubborn. You won't win any medals for proving you can run your favorite play with your best back when four defenders are keying on him.

More often than being stubborn, coaches are too willing to abandon the game plan when their team falls behind. Unless your offensive scheme is designed to strike quickly, you are likely to dig your team deeper into a hole by trying to get back in the game in a hurry.

 PUP FOR TOP PRIZE

While attending the University of Colorado's spring practice session in 1990 (a few months after the Buffaloes lost the national championship in the Orange Bowl), I noticed Bill McCartney was using a new drill. He called it PUP, Pass Under Pressure. They ran through a PUP period during each practice. PUP is something like a 2-minute drill run over and over.

Bill knew that to get to the very top, his team would need to be able to throw the ball when necessary. By preparing his team with the PUP period, Bill could make a minor rather than a major adjustment in the team's game plan when it needed to move the ball quickly with the pass.

As you know, Colorado won the Orange Bowl and the national championship that season. The PUP period paid off.

Halftime

Regardless of the score, I try to stick to business during halftime. The coaching staff asks each player how the guy across from him is playing, what he is doing, what the player thinks will work, and what the problem is with things that aren't working. We combine this feedback with our own perspective to make the adjustments we think will help. We try to stay factual and away from emotional appeals.

Probably the most significant change we make in the game plan at halftime is that we narrow our play selection. Now that we know what options aren't available, we won't waste our time trying to make them work. The players often are helpful in determining what will and won't work.

 BEWARE THE FLY SWATTER

During halftime of a game in my first year at Augustana, we were trying to figure out with our team how to handle the opponent's much bigger defensive line, which had dominated the line of scrimmage throughout the first half. More specifically, the opponent's huge defensive tackle had manhandled whomever tried to block him.

Whenever the guard positioned across from him would pull, the big tackle was through the hole and to the ballcarrier before we knew it. So we emphasized to our fullback the importance of filling the hole and blocking the massive lineman. The fullback looked at me helplessly and said, "I hate to say this, coach, but that big guy is swattin' me off like a fly."

What was I going to say to that? He was right. And his remark surely destroyed my emotional plea to correct the problem.

The opposing coach's halftime adjustments are no concern. If you start getting caught up in the "if they do this" thinking, you lose sight of what works for you. Whatever you do, don't overreact. You'll do more harm than good.

 THE WRONG APPROACH

The first program I took over hadn't won a game in a couple years. During the first game my first year there, we were behind only 13-7 at halftime, and the kids seemed a little down. So I scolded the team, thinking it would inspire the players to a better effort. Well, we went out and played terribly, and lost 52-19.

Now I realize I was whipping a beaten horse. Those kids had no belief in themselves, no confidence at all. So what I did at halftime was shoot them down even more when they needed to be built up.

The one exception where a halftime pep talk can pay off is when a team that has been a champion gets complacent. A scolding can shake the team back to reality. The emotional shock, used sparingly, can motivate such a team.

Players with high confidence and ability have a little switch; they can turn it up a notch and they know it. They can go out and play with more intensity. That may make the difference in the second half.

The Closing Minutes

"It's not over 'til it's over" could be better stated "It's not over until you let it be over." We like to play and substitute as many players as we can each week. We've put as many as 100 different players into a game. We expect each of them to give 100% effort, regardless of the score.

It doesn't make any difference whether you lose by 1 point or 30 points. What makes a difference is when your players develop a quitter's mentality. If they start giving up when it looks like it's over and it's not, they are going to miss some opportunities to come back. Opponents will learn that if they get your team down early, they have a good chance to win.

 COMEBACK KIDS

During our first national championship year, we came from behind in three of the last four playoff games against the best teams in the country. Our players on that team had an unwavering belief that we simply would not lose. Many times we stared adversity in the face and overcame it. Nothing was going to stop us. I could feel it, and so could the players.

Postgame

When the final whistle is blown, the first thing we do is congratulate the opponent. Whatever the outcome, our players and coaches have to show the sportsmanship we expect from an opponent.

In the locker room after the postgame prayer, I briefly talk with the team about the amount of effort we put into the game. We'll talk about what the outcome means to us, win or lose. We might ask the players to look ahead a little bit, to begin thinking about the team we'll play the following week.

After the game, you really can't say much to your team from a technical standpoint. You haven't seen the film yet, so to evaluate or judge their execution is ridiculous. And because I also am recovering from the emotions of the game, it is not a good time to express my perceptions of their performances.

If we have lost, I try not to make it a crushing thing. The team feels bad enough about losing anyway, so for me to carry on about it would be counterproductive.

A team needs its coach most after a loss. That doesn't mean you have to say a lot. In fact, sometimes the least said the better. But you need to be their example and to set the emotional tone.

If we win, I congratulate the team for what it did as a group. Then, I make an effort to go around and congratulate the boys individually for a job well done. I might also check their physical status and encourage them to get injuries checked by the medical staff. We tell players to enjoy the win and to be ready to come back to work on Monday.

With all the victories we've had and the businesslike approach we emphasize, our postgame locker room isn't real wild. In fact, sometimes I find myself wishing that the players would show more happiness after a great performance.

 "HEY, GUYS, WE WON!"

After winning one Saturday afternoon, I remember going into the locker room and thinking, "Hey, you guys, we won. Why aren't you more excited?" Then I realized that because everyone had expected them to win, the players didn't feel they had accomplished that much. That was wrong—that shouldn't happen, no matter how successful the program is.

Summary

1. In addition to the game plan, consider game site, the weather, and how motivated your players are in your pregame preparation.

2. Use whichever motivational aides best suit your team's temperament.
3. Your players will reflect you, so keep your concentration and composure during the game.
4. Don't abandon your system and game plan unless the time and score dictate a change.
5. Use feedback from your players during halftime to help you make adjustments you think will help in the second half.
6. Scolding a team that's losing at halftime may only make them play worse.
7. Learn to handle winning and losing with equal class and dignity.

Part VI

Coaching Evaluation

Chapter 17

Evaluating Your Players

We've all heard the media proclaim that certain coaches are "great judges of talent." But those of us who've coached know judging talent isn't so difficult, it's *finding* the talent that's the hard part.

Actually, talent assessment is just a small part of the player evaluation process. In this chapter we'll look at individual and team evaluations a football coach should make. Although player evaluation is a continual process, we'll look at the key elements of evaluating your athletes during

- off-season,
- preseason,
- practices,
- games, and
- postgames.

Individual Evaluations

The first step in evaluation is to identify your best athletes—those who have speed, those who are agile, and those who have great hands to catch the football. And identify players who have the greatest attributes for excelling in certain roles within your system.

Also look for intangible qualities that make up what we call "winners." The most important intangible is a strong desire that won't ever quit. Another prized intangible quality is character.

Each fall we have the players fill out a personal profile questionnaire. The more you know about the young men on your team, the better. Examine each player's work

157

Football Player's Personal Profile Questionnaire

Name: _____

Age: _____ Birthdate: _____ Grade: _____

Home address: _____ Phone: _____

Father's name: _____

Mother's name: _____

Father's occupation: _____

Mother's occupation: _____

Siblings' names and ages: _____

College majors: _____

Other sports you participate in at Augustana: _____

Football position played last year: _____

The position you would like to play this year: _____

Your personal goals for the football season: _____

_____

_____

How can you best help the team this year: _____

_____

_____

What time can you come in? _____

---

ethic, attitude toward other people, and personal discipline. This judgment is sometimes easier to make in smaller high school situations where you have a chance to see the athletes frequently out of school. You can also use players' performances in school—grades, attendance, behavior—to monitor how they are doing away from football.

 KNOWING YOUR PLAYERS

I remember going to a Fellowship of Christian Athletes conference years ago at which a hot topic was the individual recognition and attention we give our players.

During the conversation, the former great high school coach at Lawrence High School, Al Woolard, asked a Division I coach, "Did you ever think of putting nametags on the kids' helmets the first day of practice?"

The coach looked slightly puzzled and responded, "Why do you ask?"

Al said, "Well, when you recruit a boy, he's your long-lost friend. You put your arm around him all the time. You're super-friendly to his parents, his brother, his sister, and even his dog. Then you get him on the field and you say, 'Hey, *you,* come here.'"

The Division I coach nodded and shrugged, acknowledging that the type of individual attention given players in his program changed once they put the pads on.

The better you understand your players' tangible and intangible qualities, the better you can place the athletes with the strongest character in key positions. Correct positioning of players is critical to a football team's success. Your athletes' ability to carry out their assignments will be greatly enhanced if they are prepared and confident in their roles. In turn, your team's performance will reflect how ready and able each player is to succeed at his position.

Just one caution: Don't let one evaluation of a player influence how you perceive him during a later evaluation. Your program should be designed to improve players' athletic skills and conduct on and off the field. Young players often will develop more confidence and want to lead.

If your program has this effect, your early evaluations of players are likely to grow inaccurate as the season progresses. Other players, despite our best efforts, will slip in attitude or performance. Whatever the case, frequently reevaluate your players and make warranted changes and adjustments in personnel.

Team Evaluations

While all players deserve and need personal attention, successful football players must realize they are but a part of a group—that the team's needs must supersede those of any single player. So after you make your individual evaluations and determine where each player can most help the team, your athletes should be ready to accept their assigned role for the good of the program.

Evaluating the combined efforts of all your athletes is sometimes more difficult than individual evaluations. How do you measure the team's performance?

Do you use the easiest tool, the scoreboard? Do you look at offensive, defensive, and special team stats? Or do you check more subjective indicators, such as appraisals from the coaching staff, coaching colleagues, and fans?

To me, a team evaluation has to consider how well your team played given the talent and the game plan for that week. Did your offense and defense execute and avoid mental mistakes? Most important is whether the players played with total effort.

Satisfaction with mediocrity ensures more mediocrity. Always evaluate and strive to make your team better. If you don't, you'll get worse.

No Scoreboard Watcher

I advise against using the final score to evaluate team performance and effort. I've also said that I'm not big on statistics as a barometer. Teams that focus on holding opponents to fewer than 100 yards rushing or fewer than 12 first downs lose sight of the big picture—the overall success of the team.

No Poll Watcher

Some coaches measure their team's success by their poll rankings. That's not for me because, again, you are basing your assessment of your team on the opinions of people who don't know it as well as you do.

You can't control—or, in some ways, believe—the polls. They often look at point margins and perceived strength of schedule. Rarely do the poll voters see all of the teams, and they usually have a vested interest in the teams that they do see regularly.

  SCORE PUT IN PERSPECTIVE

In 1970, our high school team was ranked Number 1 in the state in the poll of middle-sized schools (800 to 1,300 enrollment). The next-to-last game of the season we played the Number 5 ranked team in the large school poll (1,300 students and more). The game became a state spotlight because each team, remarkably, had won 51 of its last 52 games.

It was a great, emotional game with the final score 42-6 in our favor. After the game the editor of the polling paper said that the score was the deciding factor—we would remain the state champion in the poll. My irritation with that comment led me to say that if it was the difference in score that convinced him, he should vote the Number 2 team as Number 1. The game was really a lot closer until near the end when we scored on turnovers. I also reminded him that the other undefeated school in our class could not and would not go on the field with a school as large as the one we had just beaten. He agreed, and we were the state champions. This was before Illinois had state playoffs.

Off-Season Evaluations

Between December and August is when you can focus on the talents of returning players and those entering your program. Study them in terms of how they can best fit into your system. Use film, information from position coaches and coaches at the lower levels, personal observations, and talk with the players themselves to learn about their football interest and aptitude.

This is also a time to assess and help boys trying to overcome personal problems with their schoolwork or character. Show interest in your boys beyond football. The better adjusted they are off the field, the more they'll contribute to the football program.

Off-season may be when we move a player to a different position to give him more playing time and to make us a better team. If he balks at the change, we explain our reasoning and ask him to give it his best shot in terms of preparing for the season.

We don't pencil in starters or create a depth chart during off-season. I've never believed in determining a lineup by how much weight players can bench press. We want to wait and see what players do when they take the practice field in the preseason.

In high school we always tried to develop our senior leaders in the off-season. They needed to set the tone for next season's preparation, to show the way.

Our seniors-to-be knew that they would have first crack at the position, that an underclassman would have to beat them out for a starting slot when we opened drills. Beyond that, there were no guarantees. It's amazing how much improvement some boys made from their junior to senior year.

 NO FREEBIES FOR SENIORS

Our 1976 state championship team had nine senior starters. Our 1977 state title winner also had nine seniors in its starting lineup. Our 1978 state championship team had only five senior starters, but in August when practice began we had all seniors in starting positions.

Although strong senior leadership had been the key to our two previous state championships, we did not let that keep us from fairly evaluating the underclassmen's practice effort and performance. The seniors who dropped to second team lost their jobs on the field, not in the coach's office.

Cutting Players

As a football coach, I have never cut a player. No matter how poor his ability, I don't think it's right to deprive a boy who wants to participate and meets the requirements of the team. And as I've said, all players can learn important values through their participation. Why should I deny someone that opportunity?

Football also is a game that requires numbers. With its many positions, specialty teams, and injury toll, you need a good turnout to practice effectively.

Finally, if you cut a player, you never know if you're robbing a boy or the team. Most every coach has had a "diamond in the rough" or a "late bloomer." If you cut these players at a young age, they're not likely to try out again.

Less talented upperclassmen can add a lot to a program. We've had many seniors who despite being short on ability were the backbone of the team by their dedication and by the examples they set for other players.

 A REAL KEEPER

When I came to Augustana, we had one senior who just barely made the traveling squad. He had to play on the scout squad during the week, along with what were primarily freshmen. But what a great leader he was!

He was a senior who liked the program well enough to put his ego aside and work as hard as anyone on the scout team. He provided a great model for our freshmen, who were still thinking of themselves as all-stars (which they had been the previous year in high school).

Instead of getting down in the dumps about not playing, the freshmen were inspired by this senior, who gave it his all even though he had little chance of playing on Saturday. I always have felt his unselfish attitude helped us tremendously in building our program to the level we eventually reached.

Practice Evaluations

By now you know how much I value practice. "You play like you practice" is more than a cliche to me. It's the truth.

Therefore, players' performance and effort each day in practice are very important in my evaluation. They must show progress toward the game. If you prepare and organize your practice effectively (chapter 6), you should see your players improve their readiness.

Does your defense read the scout team offense better on Thursday than it did on Wednesday? Do your offensive linemen block more efficiently and correctly later in the week? Is the mental focus of your team better on Friday than it was on Tuesday?

If your practices don't facilitate these improvements, you're planning your practices poorly. Maybe it's you, not the players, who needs evaluating.

Game Evaluations

Any football coach knows that what the naked eye sees happening on the field during a game is not always accurate. Even if you have coaches in the press box, you can determine only so much during a contest.

One thing that really helps a coach evaluate from the sidelines during a game is calling the offensive and defensive plays. When you know ahead of time what play was called, you can focus on the area and make adjustments. If you have to react to recognizing the play and then focus, you will lose time in seeing the play's execution.

On game day, about the only thing you can definitely measure is your teams' effort and enthusiasm. Look at your players as they warm up. Watch how fast they run onto and off the field. Look at how the offensive line approaches the line of scrimmage. Note the crispness of the offensive backfield's execution and of the receivers' routes. Check the authority of the defensive players' hits. Note whether the linebackers and defensive backs are responding instantly to the run and to the pass. Watch the speed with which the kicking and punting teams get downfield. Sense the players' moods on the sideline. All are indicators of your team's intensity.

Because game-day evaluation of performance is so difficult, use video to help. Study the team's execution of plays and individuals' performance of specific techniques. Watch each play until you can determine why it did or did not succeed. Break your video analyses down into macro (team) and micro (player).

Use this game film information wisely to correct and teach players. Not only will this make them better football players, but you can bet if your next opponent sees the same weaknesses in your team on the video, it will exploit them.

Postgame Evaluations

Meaningful postgame study of its performance is vital to any football program's continued success. By meaningful, I don't mean just looking at the final score or statistics. I mean looking beyond the obvious—what any fan could see—and examining the *causes* of the score and the statistics. As I said, you can accomplish this through videotape analysis.

After the game, only the players truly know how well they did. You're probably still emotionally involved in the the game and aren't as analytical as you will be later. Therefore, until you watch the game video closely, you're better off to withhold any serious evaluation about the team's performance.

Summary

Successful football coaches don't make off-hand judgments about their players or their team. They evaluate closely, interpret the information, then take the necessary action. Here are the specific points emphasized on player evaluation in this chapter:

1. Individual evaluation is continual, beginning with an examination of who your best athletes are and how they best fit into your offensive or defensive schemes.
2. Team evaluation involves looking at how all the parts function as a unit. Don't allow one individual to disrupt the smooth operation of the rest of the team.
3. One of the most important things to look for in off-season evaluations is how well your seniors-to-be assume leadership roles. This often determines what kind of season you'll have next fall.
4. The most important evaluation you make after practice is determining if your team made progress in preparing for the next game.
5. The only true determination possible during a game is whether your team was mentally and physically prepared to play.
6. Postgame is not the time to give players, media, or fans emotion-filled remarks or highly specific comments about execution. Wait until you've calmed down and studied the game video before evaluating individual and team performance.

Chapter 18

Evaluating Your Program

In addition to the careful evaluation we make of our players, we must monitor our program's overall health. This is critical, because if parts of our operation slip, that will be reflected on the field.

Even after a successful season, program evaluation is necessary. You can't stand pat. You have to anticipate problems and always look for areas that need strengthening. As we know, football coaches don't have to look very long or hard to find parts of their programs to improve. If your program is in really bad shape, you need to get help.

As a guide for program evaluation and prescription, I recommend looking at the very best football programs our sport has known.

You can become the best only if you follow examples provided by the best.

Evaluating Champion Programs

Study the great dynasties of sport and the first thing you learn is there is no doubt who is in charge. Whether it was the Packers of the '60s, the Crimson Tide of the '70s, or Nittany Lions of the '80s, there's no doubt who was running the show.

The second thing you learn from studying dynasties is that great unity, teamwork, and cooperation are essential. When you go back to the great New York Yankee dynasty, you realize how the players depended upon each other.

 SENSE OF CONFIDENCE

I can remember reading about a World Series game when San Francisco was facing the Yankee team that included Elston Howard, Roger Maris, Mickey Mantle, and Bob Richardson. After one game, the press and fans were second-guessing whether the Giants had blown the game by holding a runner at third base when it appeared he could score to win the series. Giant great Willie McCovey was up next, so the Giants chose not to gamble. The Yankees retired McCovey and won the game and the World Series.

Afterward, Elston Howard was quoted as saying, "If [the runner at third] would have tried to score, Bobby would have thrown him out. No question my teammate would have done his job and got him out." It is that type of confidence players must have to have a top-notch program.

Next, you learn from great dynasties to have great respect for the rules and great respect for each individual. Too many people look for the quick way, take short cuts, and wind up with bad characters in their program because they seek the easy way out. Sure, it's probably quicker to buy some great players, but how long will that program sustain itself? Such coaches may get rich, but they have only short-term success or have players who are always in trouble. That is not by accident.

On the other hand, some coaches don't win as much as they apparently could. You look at them and ask why they they don't have a better record with their great knowledge of the game. They know their Xs and Os inside and out, so why don't they win? Again, it's that intangible backbone of the program—the philosophy—that may be missing.

Evaluating Your Own Program

As I said in chapter 17, the most important individual evaluation that any athlete or coach makes is the honest look each of us takes at ourself. It is essential that each of us do this frequently.

Look at yourself, your staff, your team, and your opponents as honestly as possible. See the strengths and the weaknesses. Then look for the answers for improvement.

Sometimes what you find can be painful. And the decisions you may have to make in the best interest of the program can be even more painful. But in a team situation, you can have no sacred cows if you expect to succeed.

Player Feedback

Players can be great teachers for you if you watch and listen. Through their actions and words they'll give you insight into what is and isn't working; where you failed to communicate effectively; whether they are conditioned well enough or perhaps have overtrained; and whether they feel a sense of enthusiasm about and loyalty to the program.

Of one thing you can be certain: If there's a problem, your players will know it before you do. And you and your coaching staff will have to play a role in correcting it.

A team with good leadership will correct itself if internal problems arise. As the coach, you will usually hear about the problems after the season. The less you have to discipline a squad for personal problems, the better your team will perform.

Keep the doors open. No one has all the solutions. On a team, everyone wins or loses together. Impress this upon your players so they will be honest and constructive in bringing problems or solutions to you.

At the end of the season, seek out the players' evaluation of the program and its various parts. You might do this both informally through individual and group meetings and formally through a written questionnaire like the one presented on the right.

Coaching Staff Feedback

I've been blessed with a great staff. We are friends, which means we share ideas and work together very well. We've been together a long time.

It's vital your staff be honest with one another and with the players. No one should be afraid to bring up problems—real or perceived.

Name (optional) _____

Program Evaluation Form for Players

Please complete each of the following questions. Be as honest and constructive as possible. Your input into this football program is essential for its future success.

1. In terms of football skills and strategies, I learned...

1	2	3	4	5	6	7
nothing						a lot

2. My performance of football skills and strategies improved...

1	2	3	4	5	6	7
not at all						a lot

3. I enjoyed playing football this season.

1	2	3	4	5	6	7
not at all						a lot

4. The coaching staff helped me develop as a player.

1	2	3	4	5	6	7
not at all						a lot

5. The coaching staff helped me develop as a person.

1	2	3	4	5	6	7
not at all						a lot

6. Players are treated fairly on the team.

1	2	3	4	5	6	7
not at all						a lot

7. Players on the team respected team rules.

1	2	3	4	5	6	7
not at all						very true

8. Practices were well organized, challenging, and fun.

1	2	3	4	5	6	7
not at all						very true

9. The role I played in games was the best for the program.

1	2	3	4	5	6	7
not at all						very true

10. I feel more positively about the program now than I did at the beginning of the season.

1	2	3	4	5	6	7
not at all						very true

The best thing about being a player in this football program:

_____

The worst thing about being a player in this football program:

_____

Explain changes you would make to improve or eliminate the worst things about the program (be specific):

_____

_____

What can the coaching staff do to make the program better than it was this past season?

_____

_____

Additional comments (use reverse side):

Throughout the season you'll discuss day-to-day and game-to-game evaluations with your staff. But you really should take some time at the end of the season to look at the total picture. Is the staff working well together? Is each member of the staff being used in a way that best serves the program? Is everyone on the staff satisfied with their roles?

If only one staff member is dissatisfied, it may be best for that coach to leave. His continued presence might be even less enjoyable for him and more counterproductive to the program the next year. On the other hand, if several coaches indicate dissatisfaction, perhaps the head coach is communicating poorly or delegating inappropriately.

Peer evaluations, in which each member of the staff is evaluated by the other members, can be helpful if staff members make their evaluations in the spirit of improving the program rather than for personal or professional gain.

Look For the Positive

As you examine your program critically, note the good as well as the bad. Even the harshest critics—if they are fair—cite positives in their review. A balanced perspective is necessary for an accurate assessment.

 MAKING MOST OF WHO'S AVAILABLE

After our undefeated 1966 season, we returned both of our All-State running backs, Barry Pear-

son and Steve Penny. We had great backs but no line, so we decided to take our best and quickest athletes from our sophomore team and make them linemen. We then played "home run" football, using our quickness and speed for big plays. The results were an undefeated team in 1967 and an average halftime score of 27-0. In 1968, we used two linemen from the 1967 team as fullback and tailback.

Highlighting the positive is also important in building the program for the future. In other words, you can't just focus on the problems (what you don't want to do) if you expect to improve. You must also identify what works well (what you want to continue to do) and determine how to strengthen those aspects.

Sometimes, strengths and weaknesses can be addressed simultaneously. For example, if you have great support from the student body and community but your practice facilities are inadequate, invite your boosters to open practices (strengthening their support of the program) and make them aware of the your team's facility problem. Who knows, this might prompt some fund-raising activities to improve the practice site.

However you decide to evaluate, avoid making one part of the program the scapegoat for all of your problems. If you do, you'll probably miss many other areas that need your attention and overlook positive elements. And your negative obsession is not likely to get any better until you quit griping about it and do something about it!

The easiest thing in the world is to blame a player, a coach, an administrator, lack of funds, or poor facilities for unpleasant things your evaluation reveals. Instead, take the information you gather and seek *possible* solutions. If an area needs shoring up, take on the challenge of doing it. After all, that's what you ask your players to do. We would all like perfect facilities and an unlimited budget, but as in other parts of life, we must learn to do all we can with what we have.

Recordkeeping

When you say "record" to a football coach, most think of team's victories and losses. And there's no denying that the ratio of Ws to Ls will be part of your postseason evaluation.

But it's important to get beyond that in your total evaluation. If your team went 5-5, it might be on the rise or on the skids. An 8-2 team might have underachieved. A 2-8 team might have maximized its potential and built a solid base for future improvement.

Other statistics can be equally deceiving. Does it mean much if you had 30 more first downs than your opponents? Perhaps they scored on long runs and passes and didn't bother moving the chains before they scored!

Stats can help you evaluate your program, but only if they are interpreted wisely. Look at what you were trying to accomplish during the season (your goals), take the information from your evaluation of opponents' strengths and weaknesses, and then determine which statistics are meaningful to your program. If your program is closer to your goal(s) than it was at the end of the previous season, you can feel like you've made progress.

 STARTING FROM THE BOTTOM

In 1962, when we began our high school program, I was the third head football coach at the school in the last 3 years. Over the two previous seasons, the varsity had produced a dismal 1-17 record. We were hoping to win two games, just to start a positive attitude. Fortunately, we won four games the first year and established an attitude. We won six games in 1964, eight games in 1965, and then did not lose again for six years. But even though we reached the top, we never forgot where we started and what it took to improve.

Take injuries into account during this part of your evaluation. Perhaps a lack of progress stems from several key players missing practices or games. If so, consider what you can do to prevent similar injuries from recurring next season. Discuss injury reports with your sports medicine staff. Develop off-season conditioning programs for the team. Don't wait for more injuries to happen next season and then say that "things would be better if we could just stay healthy."

Building for the Future

As you evaluate, in the back of your mind remember that you either get better or worse, you don't stay the same. Football is always changing and so are your players.

Take what you learn from your postseason evaluation and apply it optimally to the situation your program will face the next season. No matter how successful your past season was, next year everyone will ask, "What have you done for me lately?"

What have you done lately, or better still, what has coaching football done for you? As a college student (100 years ago), I first thought I wanted to be an engineer. But after my first 2 years at a liberal arts college, I knew I wanted to coach. My concerns then remain today—that so many coaches lose their jobs and really are not well compensated financially for all the personal ridicule they received.

My high school coach, Leo Cabalka, was the man who sort of took me under his wing after my father passed away. So I went home and discussed my concerns with Leo. I will never forget his words. He said, "Bob, you are right. You will never get rich coaching, but I can assure you that you will never find a job you will like better and that will be as rewarding in other ways."

With all the good things that have happened to me in the coaching profession, surely God put me in the right place, and the true meaning of Coach Cabalka's words are still loud and clear to me.

Evaluating Your Position

If you are a candidate for a job, by all means be yourself. Never try to get hired by telling people what you think they want to hear. For instance, you can't say, "I run the Wing-T at school X, but I'm looking to really open it up with a pro set at school Z." If you start trying to tell others what you think they want to hear, you'll get caught in a lie and lose whatever credibility you have. That's what I meant earlier about shooting straight with everyone. Be yourself, and let the administration decide if you're the right guy.

 ON BEING HONEST

We tell children, "If you tell the truth all the time, then you will always tell the same story and won't have to remember what story you told the last time." The same is true for adults. If instead of shooting straight you tell one person one thing and another something different, they may compare notes and find you out. Or you may forget what story you told which person. In either case you've created an unnecessary dilemma because you didn't start out with the truth.

You have to be honest and hope to be accepted. Simply try to sell those considering you on your coaching philosophy; then leave it to them to decide whether they prefer your philosophy over another candidate's. Some coaches are willing to sell their souls for certain positions, or so it seems.

A coach at one of the most prestigious colleges in the country recently did that. He sold his soul, doing everything possible to get the job he'd always wanted, but then suffered the embarrassment of failing worse than anyone who had ever coached at that school. If you're not ready, you're not sure you can do the job, or you don't want to pay the price to do it justice, stay where you are.

Some research about the job may help. Knowing things like what style the school has used, what type of players you would have, and who you have to beat may impress the administration. It shows that you're really interested. You can't make any concrete decisions from such research, but it is helpful for your own information base and good for public relations. It's the same as preparing for any interview you might have, in any business. You need background knowledge to speak effectively about what you would do in the position.

On the other hand, don't worry too much about what the school has done in the past. I wouldn't watch a lot of film, except perhaps of the opponents you'll be facing. You don't want to prejudge the players who are coming back; wait and judge them on how they play for you in your system.

It might also help to network with other coaches about the position you're considering, although I always preferred to just go and look the situation over for myself. Then if I had the opportunity to decide, I could always be independent to turn it down if I saw something I didn't like.

   JOB BY DEFAULT

The first job I took, I think I took because nobody else would. The program was really poor and had a long losing streak. But I wanted the job so bad, I wanted to be head coach so bad, I was willing to take anything. Sure, I still thought it out; but I was young and foolish, and I thought we would win. We did win, but I often wonder whether I would have had all that time to devote to the school if I'd had a family.

Levels of Coaching

I could be equally happy at Augustana or Geneseo. Coaching is coaching, on any level that you experience it. The problem many coaches run into, and why they fail to ever really establish a base, is being too busy worrying about the ladder, about coaching at a bigger high school, at a major college, or in the pros.

The competitive nature of human beings is to always want to try another level, to see how you stack up. The nature of athletes is the same. An athlete always wants to test himself. I wonder how many guys getting out of college would just love a chance to try at pro ball and find out if they could or couldn't play. And it's the same with coaching. I think all of us would like to see how we could do at the next rung on the ladder. But you do the players on your team a disservice if you're not focusing on the present, giving them the best opportunity they have to be successful.

There isn't any coach who wouldn't love the challenge of standing across the sideline from a Ken Hatfield or a LaVell Edwards. It doesn't mean you would be successful the same way, but you would like to find out how you'd do. It's like that question, Why do you climb the mountain? Because it's there. Why do coaches seek more challenging positions? Because they are there—because they are challenging.

My advice is to do all you can with what you have where you are. Don't sit looking at other programs saying, "Boy, if I had his material [or, if I was at Notre Dame], I could win the national championship." That's a terrible mistake some coaches make: They worry so much about what others have that they don't focus on making their own programs the best they can be.

No coach can win them all; somewhere along the line you're going to have a setback. And even the properly focused coach at some point questions whether a particular loss or a sub-.500 season record will hurt his career. It won't, if you're doing things the right way. Everyone will recognize that it was a blip in the screen, an exception.

All any football coach can do, no matter where he is, is as well as he can. You go on from there. People have asked me about the pressure of keeping some of our long winning streaks going. I really never felt it. Sure, I want our team to be successful on Friday night, Saturday, whenever we are playing. But I also know the pressure will not change. I'm going to do just as well as I can every week, and if that's not good enough then I suspect somebody else will take my job and do better, or he'll soon be gone too. The most important thing to me throughout so-called pressure games or winning streaks is being sure I will do as well as I can. That's the key.

If you do all you can and still fail, you can at least hold your head up and walk out. But if you end saying, "I wish I had scouted them," or "I wish I would have done this or that" then you have to second-guess. The same is true in business. The business-person must ask, "Did I do everything possible to put the deal together?" Perhaps he played golf Thursday afternoon and maybe lost a sale because of that and now has to be asking "what ifs." But you would still like to think you have done everything you could.

Career Objectives

Is your objective to get the most prestigious head coaching position in the country? If that's it, then go for it. But be prepared to fall short. On the other hand, if your ambition is to simply stay in your present position and not change, then don't say that you *could* have had this job or that if you wanted it.

A funny thing about our competitive nature was impressed upon me when I was talking to Mike White about Howard Schnellenberger's lifetime contract offer from the U.S.F.L. I was joking with Mike, telling him he ought to do something like that and coach till retirement for $100,000 a year. But we both realized he couldn't, because Mike has to feel that competition, that struggle for life every weekend. That kind of contract would have gone against his competitive nature. It would have taken some of the thrill out of

coaching if the score didn't matter. And I think a lot of coaches couldn't just wait a contract out, so it is amazing that so many have that one big long-term contract as a dream. One of the greatest, Woody Hayes, had more than 20 1-year contracts at Ohio State.

The size or glamour of the school is often not as important as the economic benefits and security. And if you should be a father responsible for being a primary wage earner in a family, I believe you owe it to your wife and children to take the best opportunity available if it is a position that is consistent with your values.

I could still be happy coaching at the high school level, but I felt the move to Augustana was best for me and my family. I thought it all out, and decided to come to Augustana College for these two reasons:

* *To show that my approach could be equally successful in collegiate football.* Because of the unusual success that I enjoyed in high school football, I wanted to see if the system would work somewhere else. I believed strongly in what we did, yet I was curious whether it would work at the college level, where it had never worked before. I felt the opportunity at a small college would let me show that my approach was a sound one and could work at that level.

* *To do what was best for my family.* I have a very large family. And because Augustana offers tuition waivers to children of all of its faculty, I could afford to educate my children at a very good college if they chose to go on to school. Although any job I would ever take would have to be a greater professional challenge, more importantly it would have to be a better situation for my family and for the coaching staff that I feel responsible for.

Summary

This closing chapter described evaluations every good football program makes at the end of the season. Here are some of the key points that were presented:

1. Study the great programs and use them as prototypes to help you evaluate and improve your own program.
2. "To thine own self be true." Be honest in your appraisal of yourself, your staff, and your team.
3. Seek out valuable input from players and coaching colleagues about your program's health.

4. Be tough but optimistic in your evaluation. Don't be afraid to find the bad; if you do, develop positive solutions.
5. Always look ahead. Fame is fleeting in athletics, so don't get too satisfied with your program. Enjoy your successes, work through your failures, and always remember that you are part of a great game—football.

Sample Preseason Practice Plan

	W 25	Th 26	F 27	S 28	Su 29	M 30	T 31
		No pads					
Stretching	P	✓•	✓•	✓•	N	✓•	✓•
Conditioning stations	H	✓•	✓•	✓	O	✓	✓
Kicking	Y						
Punt	S	✓•	✓•	✓•	P	✓•	✓•
Punt cover	I	✓•	✓•	✓•	R	✓•	✓•
Punt return	C	✓	✓•	✓•	A	✓•	✓
Kickoff	A				C		•
Kickoff cover	L			✓•	T	✓•	✓•
Return					I		•
Extra point					C		✓•
Individual drills (line/backs)	F	✓•	✓•	✓•	E	✓•	✓•
Group drills—offense	I	•	✓•	✓•		✓•	✓•
Wing-T series	T	•	✓•	✓•		✓•	✓•
Inside belly	N		✓•	✓•		✓•	✓•
Outside belly	E		✓•	✓•		✓•	✓•
Trap series	S					✓•	✓•
Play-action passes	S						✓•
Dropback passes							•
Group drills—defense	T						
Position	E	•	✓•	✓•		✓•	✓•
Slant	S	•	✓•	✓•		✓•	✓•
Stunts	T	•	✓•	✓•		✓•	✓•
Coverage		•	✓•	✓•		✓•	✓•
Team practice							
Huddle		✓•	✓•	✓•		✓•	✓•
Lineup (formations)		✓•	✓•	✓•		✓•	✓•
Scrimmage (passive)			✓•	✓•		✓•	✓•
Scrimmage (live)				✓•		✓•	✓•
Game scrimmage							

Note. Due to some late classes, we also run what we call a prepractice for 10 to 15 minutes (for example, 3:30 - 3:45). During this time, the offense runs pass patterns against a skeleton defense. The position coaches work and talk with their groups about what to expect for the day. During practices the week before our first game, all of our group work is directed to our opponent for the week. ✓ = a.m.; • = p.m.

September

	W 1	Th 2	F 3	S 4	Su 5	M 6
Stretching	✓•	✓•	✓•	•	N	•
Conditioning stations	✓	✓	✓	•	O	•
Kicking						
Punt	✓•	✓•	✓•			•
Punt cover	✓•	✓•	✓•		P	•
Punt return	✓•	•	✓•		R	•
Kickoff		✓			A	•
Kickoff cover		✓			C	•
Return		✓			T	•
Extra point	•	•			I	•
Individual drills (line/backs)	✓•	✓•	✓•	•	C	•
Group drills—offense	✓•	✓•	✓•		E	•
Wing-T series	✓•	✓•				•
Inside belly	✓•	✓•	✓•			•
Outside belly	✓•	✓•	✓•			•
Trap series	✓•	✓•				•
Play-action passes	✓•	✓•	✓•			•
Dropback passes	✓•	✓•	✓•			
Group drills—defense						
Position	✓	✓•	✓•			•
Slant	✓	✓•	✓•			•
Stunts	✓	✓•	✓•			•
Coverage	✓	✓•	✓•			•
Team practice						
Huddle	✓	✓•	✓•			•
Lineup (formations)	✓	✓•	✓•			•
Scrimmage (passive)	✓	✓•	✓•			•
Scrimmage (live)	✓	✓•	✓•			•
Game scrimmage				•		

Note. Due to some late classes, we also run what we call a prepractice for 10 to 15 minutes (for example, 3:30 - 3:45). During this time, the offense runs pass patterns against a skeleton defense. The position coaches work and talk with their groups about what to expect for the day. During practices the week before our first game, all of our group work is directed to our opponent for the week. ✓ = a.m.; • = p.m.

T 7	W 8	Th 9	F 10	S 11
•	•	•	•	F
•	•	•		I
				R
•	•	•	•	S
•	•	•	•	T
•	•	•	•	
•	•	•	•	G
•	•			A
				M
•	•	•	•	E
•	•	•		
•	•	•		
•	•	•		
•	•	•		
•	•	•		
•	•	•		
•	•	•		
•		•		
		•		
•	•	•		
•	•	•		
•	•	•		
•	•	•		
•	•	•	•	
•	•	•	•	
•	•	•		
•	•	•		

Index

About the Author

Bob Reade is the head football coach at Augustana College in Rock Island, IL, where he has won an incredible 87% of his games—the highest winning percentage of any active college football coach and second only to Knute Rockne on the all-time list.

Since Reade's arrival at Augustana in 1979, his teams have put together impressive strings of victories and championships, including 4 straight NCAA Division III national championships (1983-1986), 10 straight NCAA Division III play-off appearances (1981-1990), 8 straight conference titles (1981-1988), and a record-breaking 60 games in a row without a defeat (1983-1987). Reade's success on the field has helped him earn distinction as National Coach of the Year four times and College Conference of Illinois and Wisconsin (CCIW) Coach of the Year seven times.

Before coming to Augustana, Reade was head coach at J.D. Darnall High School in Geneseo, IL, where he built a similar football dynasty. In 17 years, he complied a 146-21-4 record, which included a 52-game unbeaten streak and three straight Class 3A state championships. He was also named Illinois High School Coach of the Year four times.

In addition to coaching football, Reade teaches physical eduction at Augustana. He is also very active in the Fellowship of Christian Athletes. Reade lives in Geneseo, IL, where he enjoys spending time with his family.